I Belong to God!

An intergenerational study guide for *By Water and the Spirit: A United Methodist Understanding of Baptism*

Carolyn K. Tanner

OSL Publications
Akron, Ohio

I Belong to God!
An intergenerational study guide for
"By Water and the Spirit: A United Methodist Understanding of Baptism"

ISBN 978-1-878009-58-6

This book is printed on acid-free paper that meets the American National Standards Institute Z39.48 Standard

Produced and manufactured in the United States of America by
OSL Publications
P O Box 22279
Akron Ohio 44302-0079

Word Search puzzles were created using *http://www.puzzle-maker.com/WS/index.htm*.

Members of the United Methodist Baptism Study Committee

Mark Trotter, Chair	John Gooch
Peggy Sewell, Secretary	Sharon Hels
Dan Benedict	Pat Jelinek
Ole Borgen	Chuck Kishpaugh
Sang E. Chun	Thomas Langford
Dale Dunlap	Jeanne Audrey Powers
John Ewing	Thomas Salsgiver
Gayle Felton	Stanley Washington
Garnett Wilder	

Contents

Introduction

In 1996 the General Conference of the United Methodist Church approved *By Water and the Spirit: A United Methodist Understanding of Baptism*. It brought a clearer understanding to the sacrament of baptism beginning with a review of the history and traditions of the Methodists, through John Wesley, and those of the Evangelical and United Brethren congregations. It continued by defining and reaffirming God's gift of grace and the sacraments of baptism and Holy Communion as special means or channels of grace given to all.

Since any one of any age can be baptized, it follows that a study of baptism could also include those of all ages. Followers of Jesus have been touched by the Holy Spirit and they experience God's grace as they learn and grow together. The sessions in this intergenerational study guide include the full text of *By Water and the Spirit: A United Methodist Understanding of Baptism* and are divided into six sessions. Each session includes teaching plans to use as an intergenerational gathering, following the pattern; Step into Learning, Opening Worship, Take a Close Look, Learn by Doing, and a Time of Sharing and Worship.

The question-and-response portion of each session's opening worship is designed to complement and reinforce material from *Baptism in The United Methodist Church*: A Companion DVD to "By Water and the Spirit." Nashville, United Methodist Productions/EcuFilm, 2007. We commend the DVD for your use.

Keep in mind that it is not necessary to plan and to fill every moment of your time together with direct instruction and activities. Encourage moments of quiet to further deepen the grace God offers. Let there be time for meditation, for growth and understanding to capture the soul as grace and love surround all who gather. Use the ideas included in this guide in ways that are fitting for your gathering, expecting those enriching quiet moments.

There are several ways in which this intergenerational guide can be a useful study. Use it for a Sunday morning or a weekday class; add an active game and a snack to use it for Vacation Bible School, add study time preceding or following congregational suppers, bring the whole congregation together as a way to receive the grace of God.

The study guide also includes a substantial appendix, which includes the song from which the study derives its name, a full complement of suggestions for the Learn by Doing activities, word search puzzle suggestions and other material you may find helpful in your teaching. Material from the appendix that may be photocopied is indicated by the permissions notice at the bottom of those pages.

May your study be blessed as you and your students learn more about the gift of baptism!

Carolyn K. Tanner

Where Are We?
How Did We Get Here?

Contemporary United Methodism is attempting to recover and revitalize its understanding of baptism. To do this, we must look to our heritage as Methodists and Evangelical United Brethren and, indeed, to the foundations of Christian Tradition. Throughout our history, baptism has been viewed in diverse and even contradictory ways. An enriched understanding of baptism, restoring the Wesleyan blend of sacramental and evangelical aspects, will enable United Methodists to participate in the sacrament with renewed appreciation for this gift of God's grace.

Within the Methodist tradition, baptism has long been a subject of much concern, even controversy. John Wesley retained the sacramental theology which he received from his Anglican heritage. He taught that in baptism a child was cleansed of the guilt of original sin, initiated into the covenant with God, admitted into the Church, made an heir of the divine kingdom, and spiritually born anew. He said that while baptism was neither essential to nor sufficient for salvation, it was the "ordinary means" that God designated for applying the benefits of the work of Christ in human lives.

On the other hand, although he affirmed the regenerating grace of infant baptism, he also insisted upon the necessity of adult conversion for those who have fallen from grace. A person who matures into moral accountability must respond to God's grace in repentance and faith. Without personal decision and commitment to Christ, the baptismal gift is rendered ineffective.

Baptism for Wesley, therefore, was a part of the lifelong process of salvation. He saw spiritual rebirth as a twofold experience in the normal process of Christian development—to be received through baptism in infancy and through commitment to Christ later in life. Salvation included both God's initiating activity of grace and a willing human response.

Session One

Teaching Plans

LESSON FOCUS: Baptism identifies us as people for whom Jesus Christ lived, died, and was resurrected.

GENERAL SUPPLIES NEEDED: You will want to have large sheets of paper and markers available during each session. Supplies needed for *Learn by Doing* are listed on the Appendix pages.

PREPARATION NOTES: The opening worship includes a question and response. In this way the baptism topic for the session is considered. Choose those who will ask and respond. With coaching, a non-reader could ask the question. The one responding needs to be competent in reading and speaking. It could be a youth, older child, or an adult. Give both individuals time to prepare. Supply a visual means to identify those two, such as scarves, head bands, sashes, etc.

Display the lesson focus in your room. You may wish to make a poster, adding each session's focus as the study progresses (see Appendix page 65).

There are several opportunities during the session for music. Have someone prepared to lead.

Prepare a simple gathering area for beginning and ending each session and for any necessary announcements. Include a cross and,

1

if possible, your congregation's baptismal font or supply a large shell. You might want to have electric or battery candles that can safely be left lit during the entire session.

Display pictures with a baptismal theme. You may have some in the picture files at your church or you may locate some online.

Prepare and have available paper/pencil/coloring sheets for use as needed at any time during the session. A word search puzzle for each session is available in the Appendix or create your own at *www.puzzlemaker.com* using the words listed on the appropriate Appendix page. The puzzle could be a cooperative time for older and younger learners. Coloring pages can be created using clip art. Look for images such as baptismal fonts, shells, boats, doves, etc.

For infants and toddlers, provide water toys. You may ask parents or others to bring in items such as a water mat, plastic toy aquarium, water crib toys, toy waterfall, bath toys, bath mitts, hooded bath towels, a water play center, beach toys, water flutes or whistles, water babies (dolls to fill with warm water). Provide appropriate safety precautions and supervision.

Do you need name tags? Make sure that everyone has one, youngest to oldest!

STEP INTO LEARNING: *God Created.*
Ask participants to take seats in a circle as they arrive. Designate one person as leader, who addresses each one in the circle individually saying, "[*Name,*] and God created." Each individual responds by naming something (plant, animal, elements of

In its development in the United States, Methodism was unable to maintain this Wesleyan balance of sacramental and evangelical emphases. Access to the sacraments was limited during the late eighteenth and early nineteenth centuries when the Methodist movement was largely under the leadership of laypersons who were not authorized to administer them. On the American frontier where human ability and action were stressed, the revivalistic call for individual decision-making, though important, was subject to exaggeration. The sacramental teachings of Wesley tended to be ignored. In this setting, while infant baptism continued not only to be practiced, but also to be vigorously defended, its significance became weakened and ambiguous.

Later toward the end of the nineteenth century, the theological views of much of Methodism were influenced by a new set of ideas which had become dominant in American culture. These ideas included optimism about the progressive improvement of humankind and confidence in the social benefits of scientific discovery, technology, and education. Assumptions of original sin gave way before the assertion that human nature was essentially unspoiled. In this intellectual milieu, the old evangelical insistence upon conversion and spiritual rebirth seemed quaint and unnecessary.

Thus the creative Wesleyan synthesis of sacramentalism and evangelicalism was torn asunder and both its elements devalued. As a result, infant baptism was variously interpreted and often reduced to a ceremony of dedication. Adult baptism was sometimes interpreted as a profession of faith and public acknowledgment of God's grace, but was more often viewed simply as an act of joining the Church. By the middle of the twentieth century, Methodism in general had ceased to understand baptism as authentically sacramental. Rather than an act of divine grace, it was seen as an expression of human choice.

Baptism was also a subject of concern and controversy in the Evangelical and United Brethren traditions that were brought together in 1946 in The Evangelical United Brethren Church. Their early pietistic revivalism, based upon belief in the availability of divine grace and the freedom of human choice, emphasized bringing people to salvation through Christian experience. In the late nineteenth and early twentieth centuries, both Evangelical and United Brethren theologians stressed the importance of baptism as integral to the proclamation of the gospel, as a rite initiating persons into the covenant community (paralleling circumcision), and as a sign of the new birth, that gracious divine act by which persons are redeemed from sin and reconciled to God. The former Evangelical Church consistently favored the baptism of infants. The United Brethren provided for the baptism of both infants and adults. Following the union of 1946, The Evangelical United Brethren Church adopted a ritual that included services of baptism for infants and adults, and also a newly created service for the dedication of infants that had little precedent in official rituals of either of the former churches.

The 1960-64 revision of *The Methodist Hymnal*, including rituals, gave denominational leaders an opportunity to begin to recover the sacramental nature of baptism in contemporary Methodism. The General Commission on Worship sounded this note quite explicitly in its introduction to the new ritual in 1964:

In revising the Order for the Administration of Baptism, the Commission on Worship has endeavored to keep in mind that baptism is a sacrament, and to restore it to the Evangelical-Methodist concept set forth in our Articles of Religion . . . Due recognition was taken of the critical reexamination of the theology of the Sacrament of Baptism which is currently taking place in ecumenical circles, and of its theological content and implications.

The commission provided a brief historical perspective demonstrating that the understanding of baptism as a sacrament had been weakened, if not discarded altogether, over the years. Many in the Church regarded baptism, both of infants and adults, as a dedication rather than as a sacrament. The commission pointed out that in a dedication we make a gift of a life to God for God to accept, while in a sacrament God offers the gift of God's unfailing grace

weather, etc.) created by God. The leader replies, "And God said," followed by the group responding, "I like it." Continue until all have had the opportunity to contribute. (This activity is designed to reinforce the Bible story used later in the session as part of *Learning and Doing*.)

OPENING WORSHIP

· Lesson Focus: Baptism identifies us as people for whom Jesus Christ lived, died, and was resurrected.

· Light the candles: Consider saying something like: "As I light this candle let me remember - - - (It could be the same phrase each week, for example: my baptism, Jesus' baptism, God's great love for me.)

· Question: What does baptism do for us? How can I understand it?

· Response: Baptism identifies us as people for whom Jesus Christ lived, died, and was resurrected.

You may wish to say something like: "United Methodists believe that Baptism and the Lord's Supper are sacraments, ways of knowing God's presence. Baptism is very important for Christian disciples: its meanings include initiation, salvation, new birth, adoption into God's family, death and resurrection, anointing with the Holy Spirit, forgiveness of sin, washed and being cleansed, putting on Christ.

Did you count those meanings? It is a lot, even just to count. Understanding it will take your whole life. Each time we think we understand, we grow and mature more in faith; only to find that now our understanding is much deeper. It's not that one of those meanings is "more" right or "less" right than any of the others - they are all part of the meaning of baptism and cannot be separated one from another without lim-

3

iting our understanding of this special gift from God. Here is a plan – let's look at baptism together, all of us, young and old, big and little, those who wear sneakers, and those who wear cowboy boots, those in raincoats and those in snowsuits, all together and with all its many meanings. Here we go! By Water and the Spirit."

· Music: Sing "I Belong to God" (see page 41). This simple song will add much to your opening worship. Be prepared to help people learn it. Ask all to stand as you sing it through once using the suggested motions (voice – point to mouth, hands – reach forward, arms extended, eyes – point to eyes, ears – point to ears). As you sing it a second time offer an invitation for all to begin to sing with you as they feel comfortable, or to just do the motions with you. Sing a third time, again inviting others to join.

· Apostles' Creed: You might wish to point out that this creed has been associated with baptism since the early church. Choose either the Traditional or Ecumenical Version (*The United Methodist Hymnal*, 881 or 882).

· Prayer: by leader or ask for a volunteer. You might use the "Prayers of the People" (*The United Methodist Hymnal*, page 879). Conclude with The Lord's Prayer (*The United Methodist Hymnal*, 894, 895, or 896).

TAKE A CLOSE LOOK

Consider the ages of the participants and the time you have for the session as you choose the amount of reading and discussing you will do. You may want to use some of these suggestions for at home preparation or follow-up study. They are also available in the Appendix for easy copying.

for us to accept. The 1964 revision of the ritual of the sacrament of baptism began to restore the rite to its original and historic meaning as a sacrament.

In the 1989 *The United Methodist Hymnal*, the Services of the Baptismal Covenant I, II and IV (taken from the 1984 official ritual of the denomination as printed in *The Book of Services*) continue this effort to reemphasize the historic significance of baptism. These rituals, in accenting the reality of sin and of regeneration, the initiating of divine grace and the necessity of repentance and faith, are consistent with the Wesleyan combination of sacramentalism and evangelicalism.

United Methodism is not alone in the need to recover the significance of baptism nor in its work to do so. Other Christian communions are also reclaiming the importance of this sacrament for Christian faith and life. To reach the core of the meaning and practice of baptism, all have found themselves led back through the life of the Church to the Apostolic Age. An ecumenical convergence has emerged from this effort, as can be seen in the widely acclaimed document, *Baptism, Eucharist, and Ministry* (1982).

Established by the General Conference of 1988 and authorized to continue its work by the General Conference of 1992, the Committee to Study Baptism is participating in this process by offering a theological and functional understanding of baptism as embodied in the ritual of The United Methodist Church. In so doing, the broad spectrum of resources of Scripture, Christian tradition, and the Methodist-Evangelical United Brethren experience has been taken into account. The growing ecumenical consensus has assisted us in our thinking.

You may choose to read the entire portion of "By Water and the Spirit" included in Session 1 *or* read from the adjoining column the fourth paragraph beginning "Baptism for Wesley, therefore, was - - - " (page 1) *or* read from the adjoining column the last three paragraphs for the session.

Read page 32, *The United Methodist Hymnal*, "Concerning the Services of the Baptismal Covenant."

Read The Baptismal Covenant I, *The United Methodist Hymnal*, pages 33-39.

Keep a journal of your thoughts about baptism. You could begin by recording your thoughts about the focus statement: Baptism identifies us as people for whom Jesus Christ lived, died, and was resurrected.

LEARN BY DOING

Note: all of the following suggestions are designed to enhance this study of baptism. Choose to include those that fit your time and space, as well as the ages and interests of the participants. You may choose to set up learning centers (music, Bible stories, missions, water, and crafts) with a specified amount of time in each. Alternately, in each session you may plan to select several suggestions from *Learn by Doing*. Encourage all to tap into the child within and the depth of Christ in all of us. "And a child shall lead them" (Isaiah 11:6). May we grow into that which God intends!

· Music: Learn "Awesome God," (*The Faith We Sing*, p. 2040), and write a rap. For specific 'how to' suggestions and other music ideas see Appendix page 43.

· Bible Stories: Read the biblical account of the Six Days of Creation. For specific 'how to' suggestions and other creative ideas for Bible stories see Appendix page 46. If you did not use the *Step into Learning* activity suggested for the opening of the session you may want to include it here, as a way to introduce the story of creation.

· Missions: Consider the responsibility you accept in baptism. Spend some time learning about missions. For specific 'how to' suggestions see Appendix page 49.

· Water: Choose from a variety of activities to learn more about and appreciate water. For specific 'how to' suggestions see Appendix page 51.

· Crafts: Consider learning and appreciating baptism through crafts. Choose from a variety of activities. For specific 'how to' suggestions see Appendix page 53.

TIME OF SHARING AND WORSHIP

This time can be very informal, asking those who are willing to share how they have spent their time and what they learned in the *Learn by Doing* opportunities. End your time together with a simple prayer and music. Sing "I Have Decided to Follow Jesus," *The Faith We Sing,* page 2129 or "I Belong to God" (page 41).

Who Are we?
Who Does God Intend Us To Be?

We are Saved by God's Grace

The Human Condition

As told in the first chapters of Genesis, in creation God made human beings in the image of God—a relationship of intimacy, dependence, and trust. We are open to the indwelling presence of God and given freedom to work with God to accomplish the divine will and purpose for all of creation and history. To be human as God intended is to have loving fellowship with God and to reflect the divine nature in our lives as fully as possible.

Tragically, as Genesis 3 recounts, we are unfaithful to that relationship. The result is a thorough distortion of the image of God in us and the degrading of the whole of creation. Through prideful overreach or denial of our God-given responsibilities, we exalt our own will, invent our own values, and rebel against God. Our very being is dominated by an inherent inclination toward evil which has traditionally been called original sin. It is a universal human condition and affects all aspects of life. Because of our condition of sin, we are separated from God, alienated from one another, hostile to the natural world, and even at odds with our own best selves. Sin may be expressed as errant priorities, as deliberate wrongdoing, as apathy in the face of need, as cooperation with oppression and injustice. Evil is cosmic as well as personal; it afflicts both individuals and the institutions of our human society. The nature of sin is represented in Baptismal Covenants I, II and IV in *The United Methodist Hymnal* by the phrases "the spiritual forces of wickedness" and "the evil powers of this world," as well as "your sin." Before God all persons are lost, helpless to save themselves, and in need of divine mercy and forgiveness.

Session Two

Teaching Plans

LESSON FOCUS: Grace is God's free gift.

GENERAL SUPPLIES NEEDED: You will want to have large sheets of paper and markers available during each session. Supplies needed for *Learn by Doing* are listed on the Appendix pages.

PREPARATION NOTES: The opening worship includes a question and response. In this way the baptism topic for the session is considered. Choose those who will ask and respond. With coaching, a non-reader could ask the question. The one responding needs to be competent in reading and speaking. It could be a youth, older child, or an adult. Give both individuals time to prepare. Supply a visual means to identify those two, such as scarves, head bands, sashes, etc.

Display the lesson focus in your room. You may wish to make a poster, adding each session's focus as the study progresses (see Appendix page 65).

There are several opportunities during the session for music. Have someone prepared to lead.

Prepare a simple gathering area for beginning and ending each session and for any necessary announcements. Include a cross and, if possible, your congregation's baptismal font or supply a large shell.

I Belong to God!

You might want to have electric or battery candles that can safely be left lit during the entire session.

Display pictures with a baptismal theme. You may have some in the picture files at your church or you may locate some online.

Prepare and have available paper/pencil/coloring sheets for use as needed at any time during the session. A word search puzzle for each session is available in the Appendix or create your own at *www.puzzlemaker.com* using the words listed on the appropriate Appendix page. The puzzle could be a cooperative time for older and younger learners. Coloring pages can be created using clip art. Look for images such as baptismal fonts, shells, boats, doves, etc.

For infants and toddlers, provide water toys. You may ask parents or others to bring in items such as a water mat, plastic toy aquarium, water crib toys, toy waterfall, bath toys, bath mitts, hooded bath towels, a water play center, beach toys, water flutes or whistles, water babies (dolls to fill with warm water). Provide appropriate safety precautions and supervision.

Do you need name tags? Make sure that everyone has one, youngest to oldest!

STEP INTO LEARNING: *I Would Take.*
Ask participants to take seats in a circle as they arrive. Explain that the Hebrews were moving, they would be leaving the whole country. Pretend that you are one of those people getting ready to move. What would you take? Begin with, "If I were moving I would take...." Each person will take one thing, but needs

The Divine Initiative of God

While we have turned from God, God has not abandoned us. Instead, God graciously and continuously seeks to restore us to that loving relationship for which we were created, to make us into the persons that God would have us be. To this end God acts preveniently, that is, before we are aware of it, reaching out to save humankind. The Old Testament records the story of God's acts in the history of the covenant community of Israel to work out the divine will and purpose. In the New Testament story, we learn that God came into this sinful world in the person of Jesus Christ to reveal all that the human mind can comprehend about who God is and who God would have us be. Through Christ's death and resurrection, the power of sin and death was overcome and we are set free to again be God's own people (1 Peter 2:9). Since God is the only initiator and source of grace, all grace is prevenient in that it precedes and enables any movement that we can make toward God. Grace brings us to an awareness of our sinful predicament and of our inability to save ourselves; grace motivates us to repentance and gives us the capacity to respond to divine love In the words of the baptismal ritual: "All this is God's gift, offered to us without price" (*The United Methodist Hymnal*, page 33)

The Necessity of faith for Salvation

Faith is both a gift of God and a human response to God. It is the ability and willingness to say "yes" to the divine offer of salvation. Faith is our awareness of our utter dependence upon God, the surrender of our selfish wills, the trusting reliance upon divine mercy. The candidate for baptism answers "I do" to the question "Do you confess Jesus Christ as your Savior, put your whole trust in his grace, and promise to serve him as your Lord

. . . ?" (*The United Methodist Hymnal*, page 34). Our personal response of faith requires conversion in which we turn away from sin and turn instead to

God. It entails a decision to commit our lives to the Lordship of Christ, an acceptance of the forgiveness of our sins, the death of our old selves, an entering into a new life of the Spirit—being born again (John 3:3-5, 2 Corinthians 5:17). All persons do not experience this spiritual rebirth in the same way. For some, there is a singular, radical moment of conversion. For others, conversion may be experienced as the dawning and growing realization that one has been constantly loved by God and has a personal reliance upon Christ. John Wesley described his own experience by saying, "I felt my heart strangely warmed. I felt I did trust in Christ, Christ alone for salvation; and an assurance was given me that he had taken away my sins, even mine, and saved me from the law of sin and death."

The means by which God's grace comes to us

Divine grace is made available and effective in human lives through a variety of means or "channels," as Wesley called them. While God is radically free to work in many ways, the Church has been given by God the special responsibility and privilege of being the Body of Christ which carries forth God's purpose of redeeming the world. Wesley recognized the Church itself as a means of grace—a grace-filled and grace-sharing community of faithful people. United Methodism shares with other Protestant communions the understanding that the proclamation of the Word through preaching, teaching, and the life of the Church is a primary means of God's grace. The origin and rapid growth of Methodism as a revival movement occurred largely through the medium of the proclaimed Gospel. John Wesley also emphasized the importance of prayer, fasting, Bible study, and meetings of persons for support and sharing.

Because God has created and is creating all that is, physical objects of creation can become the bearers of divine presence, power, and meaning, and thus become sacramental means of God's grace. Sacraments are effective means of God's presence mediated through the created world. God becoming incarnate in Jesus Christ is the supreme instance of this kind of divine

to repeat, in the order given, all those items that others have listed before. The object is to see how many people can repeat the entire list as it grows. You might suggest that children younger than three years old wouldn't need to repeat the list but just name their item, and children between 3 and 6 years need to just repeat those they can remember. Everyone else tries for the entire list. (This activity is designed to reinforce the Bible story used later in the session as part of *Learning and Doing*.)

OPENING WORSHIP

· Lesson Focus: Grace is God's free gift.

· Light the candles: Consider saying something like: "As I light this candle let me remember - - - (It could be the same phrase each week, for example: my baptism, Jesus' baptism, God's great love for me.)

· Question: What is grace and what does it have to do with baptism?

· Response: You may wish to say something like: "Let's start with the question about grace. Very simply, it is God's love for us. We don't earn it; we don't do anything to get it. We don't even deserve it. And it is free. God loves us always and completely. God wants what is best for us. That is pretty wonderful, isn't it? Awesome! Fantastic! Tremendous!

God's love is all of that. It has everything to do with baptism. Listen to this story about the baptism of Jesus:

"Then Jesus came from Galilee to John at the Jordan, to be baptized by him. John would have prevented him, saying, 'I need to be baptized by you, and do you come to me?' But Jesus answered him, 'Let it be so now for it is proper for us in this way to fulfill all righteousness.' Then he consented. And when Jesus had been baptized, just as he came up from the water, suddenly the heavens were opened to him and he saw the Spirit of God descending like a dove and alighting on him. And a voice from heaven said, 'This is my Son, the Beloved with whom I am well pleased.'" (Matthew 3:13-17)

Jesus was baptized in the Jordan River. God let it be known that Jesus is God's son and that God loves him. Christians believe that God's love is shown to us in Jesus, and comes to us through the work of the Holy Spirit and that baptism is one way we receive it. Baptism is God's gift of love. God is reaching out and handing us a gift. The Holy Spirit is present, bringing that gift. Do you notice that there is action going on? It is not a time to only remember something from the past, it is happening now. Think about it this way; if you were to read a book about a famous person or if you saw a TV program about someone you would learn about them, probably a lot about them. But, it is much different if you actually meet that person, isn't it? In baptism, through the Holy Spirit, Jesus is really present, bringing God's love.

Is that all there is to it? Yes, and No! It has already been said, and will probably be said again, that you might think you understand it all but that doesn't happen even in a whole lifetime."

· Music: Sing "I Belong to God" (see page 41). If you are using the song for the first time, you may wish to follow the teaching suggestions from Session One (page 4).

· Apostles' Creed: You might wish to point out that this creed has been associated with baptism since the early church. Choose either the Traditional or Ecumenical Version (*The United Methodist Hymnal,* 881 or 882).

· Prayer: by leader or ask for a volunteer. You might use the "Prayers

action. Wesley viewed the sacraments as crucial means of grace and affirmed the Anglican teaching that "a sacrament is 'an outward sign of inward grace, and a means whereby we receive the same.'" Combining words, actions, and physical elements, sacraments are sign-acts which both express and convey God's grace and love. Baptism and the Lord's Supper are sacraments that were instituted or commanded by Christ in the Gospels.

United Methodists believe that these sign-acts are special means of grace. The ritual action of a sacrament does not merely point to God's presence in the world, but also participates in it and becomes a vehicle for conveying that reality. God's presence in the sacraments is real, but it must be accepted by human faith if it is to transform human lives. The sacraments do not convey grace either magically or irrevocably, but they are powerful channels through which God has chosen to make grace available to us. Wesley identified baptism as the initiatory sacrament by which we enter into the covenant with God and are admitted as members of Christ's Church. He understood the Lord's Supper as nourishing and empowering the lives of Christians and strongly advocated frequent participation in it. The Wesleyan tradition has continued to practice and cherish the various means through which divine grace is made present to us.

of the People" (*The United Methodist Hymnal*, page 879). Conclude with The Lord's Prayer (*The United Methodist Hymnal*, 894, 895, or 896).

TAKE A CLOSE LOOK

Consider the ages of the participants and the time you have for the session as you choose the amount of reading and discussing you will do. You may want to use some of these suggestions for at home preparation or follow-up study. They are also available in the Appendix for easy copying.

You may choose to read the entire portion of "By Water and the Spirit" included in Session Two or select from the following suggestions:

Read from the adjoining column the phrase immediately before the heading "The Necessity of Faith for Salvation." It begins "- - - grace motivates us to repentance - - - ." (page 8) Continue by reading the first two sentences beneath that heading *or*

Read the second and third paragraphs of the section "The Means by Which God's Grace Comes to Us" *or*

If you didn't read page 32 of *The United Methodist Hymnal* during the previous session, do so now.

· Read The Baptismal Covenant II, *The United Methodist Hymnal*, pages 39-44.

· Keep a journal of your thoughts about baptism. You could begin by recording your thoughts about the focus statement: Grace is God's free gift.

LEARN BY DOING

Note: all of the following suggestions are designed to enhance this study of baptism. Choose to include those that fit your time and space, as well as the ages and interests of the participants. You may choose to set up learning centers (music, Bible stories, missions, water, and crafts) with a specified amount of time in each. Alternately, in each session you may plan to select several suggestions from *Learn by Doing*. Encourage all to tap into the child within and the depth of Christ in all of us. "And a child shall lead them" (Isaiah 11:6). May we grow into that which God intends!

· Music: Sing "Amazing Grace," *(The United Methodist Hymnal* page 378) and add some creative motions. For specific 'how to' suggestions and other music ideas see Appendix page 43.

· Bible Stories: Read the story of the Exodus. For specific 'how to' suggestions and other creative ideas for Bible stories see Appendix page 46. If you did not use the *Step into Learning* activity suggested for the opening of the session you may want to include it here, as a way to introducing the story of the Exodus.

· Missions: Consider the responsibility you accept in baptism. Spend some time learning about missions. For specific 'how to' suggestions see Appendix page 49.

· Water: Choose from a variety of activities to learn more about and appreciate water. For specific 'how to' suggestions see Appendix page 51.

· Crafts: Consider learning and appreciating baptism through crafts. Choose from a variety of activities. For specific 'how to' suggestions see Appendix page 53.

TIME OF SHARING AND WORSHIP

This time can be very informal, asking those who are willing to share how they have spent their time and what they learned in the *Learn by Doing* opportunities. End your time together with a simple prayer and music. Sing "I Have Decided to Follow Jesus," *The Faith We Sing,* page 2129 or "I Belong to God" (page 41).

The Meaning of Baptism

Baptism & the Life of Faith

The New Testament records that Jesus was baptized by John (Matthew 3:13-17), and he commanded his disciples to teach and baptize in the name of the Father, Son, and Holy Spirit (Matthew 28:19). Baptism is grounded in the life, death, and resurrection of Jesus Christ; the grace which baptism makes available is that of the atonement of Christ which makes possible our reconciliation with God. Baptism involves dying to sin, newness of life, union with Christ, receiving the Holy Spirit, and incorporation into Christ's Church. United Methodists affirm this understanding in their official documents of faith. Article XVII of the Articles of Religion (Methodist) calls baptism "a sign of regeneration or the new birth"; the Confession of Faith (EUB) states that baptism is "a representation of the new birth in Christ Jesus and a mark of Christian discipleship."

The Baptismal Covenant

In both the Old and New Testament, God enters into covenant relationship with God's people. A covenant involves promises and responsibilities of both parties; it is instituted through a special ceremony and expressed by a distinguishing sign. By covenant God constituted a servant community of the people of Israel, promising to be their God and giving them the Law to make clear how they were to live. The circumcision of male infants is the sign of this covenant (Genesis 17:1-14, Exodus 24:1-12). In the death and resurrection of Jesus Christ, God fulfilled the prophecy of a new covenant and called forth the Church as a servant community (Jeremiah 31:31-34, 1 Corinthians 11:23-26). The baptism of infants and

Session Three

Teaching Plans

LESSON FOCUS: Baptism is the sign of the New Covenant.

GENERAL SUPPLIES NEEDED: You will want to have large sheets of paper and markers available during each session. Supplies needed for *Learn by Doing* are listed on the Appendix pages.

PREPARATION NOTES: The opening worship includes a question and response. In this way the baptism topic for the session is considered. Choose those who will ask and respond. With coaching, a non-reader could ask the question. The one responding needs to be competent in reading and speaking. It could be a youth, older child, or an adult. Give both individuals time to prepare. Supply a visual means to identify those two, such as scarves, head bands, sashes, etc.

Display the lesson focus in your room. You may wish to make a poster, adding each session's focus as the study progresses (see Appendix page 65).

There are several opportunities during the session for music. Have someone prepared to lead.

Prepare a simple gathering area for beginning and ending each session and for any necessary announcements. Include a cross and, if possible, your congregation's baptismal font or supply a large shell. You might want to have electric or battery candles that can safely be left lit during the entire session.

Display pictures with a baptismal theme. You may have some in the picture files at your church or you may locate some online.

Prepare and have available paper/pencil/coloring sheets for use as needed at any time during the session. A word search puzzle for each session is available in the Appendix or create your own at *www.puzzle-maker.com* using the words listed on the appropriate Appendix page. The puzzle could be a cooperative time for older and younger learners. Coloring pages can be created using clip art. Look for images such as baptismal fonts, shells, boats, doves, etc.

For infants and toddlers, provide water toys. You may ask parents or others to bring in items such as a water mat, plastic toy aquarium, water crib toys, toy waterfall, bath toys, bath mitts, hooded bath towels, a water play center, beach toys, water flutes or whistles, water babies (dolls to fill with warm water). Provide appropriate safety precautions and supervision.

Do you need name tags? Make sure that everyone has one, youngest to oldest!

For STEP INTO LEARNING, immediately below, you will need two umbrellas.

STEP INTO LEARNING: *Umbrella Tag.* As people arrive ask them to take a position so that they can touch either one of two umbrellas,

adults, both male and female, is the sign of this covenant.

Therefore, United Methodists identify our ritual for baptism as "The Services of the Baptismal Covenant" (*The United Methodist Hymnal*, pages 32-54). In baptism the Church declares that it is bound in covenant to God; through baptism new persons are initiated into that covenant. The covenant connects God, the community of faith, and the person being baptized; all three are essential to the fulfillment of the baptismal covenant. The faithful grace of God initiates the covenant relationship and enables the community and the person to respond with faith.

Baptism by Water and the Holy Spirit

Through the work of the Holy Spirit—the continuing presence of Christ on earth—the Church is instituted to be the community of the new covenant. Within this community, baptism is by water and the Spirit (John 3:5, Acts 2:38). In God's work of salvation, the mystery of Christ's death and resurrection is inseparably linked with the gift of the Holy Spirit given on the day of Pentecost (Acts 2). Likewise, participation in Christ's death and resurrection is inseparably linked with receiving the Spirit (Romans 6:1-11, 8:9-14). The Holy Spirit who is the power of creation (Genesis 1:2) is also the giver of new life. Working in the lives of people before, during, and after their baptisms, the Spirit is the effective agent of salvation. God bestows upon baptized persons the presence of the Holy Spirit, marks them with an identifying seal as God's own, and implants in their hearts the first installment of their inheritance as sons and daughters of God (2 Corinthians 1:21-22). It is through the Spirit that the life of faith is nourished until the final deliverance when they will enter into the fullness of salvation(Ephesians 1:13-14).

Since the Apostolic Age, baptism by water and baptism of the Holy Spirit have been connected (Acts 19:17). Christians are baptized with both, sometimes by different sign-actions. Water is administered in the name of the triune God (specified in the ritual as

Father, Son, and Holy Spirit) by an authorized person and the Holy Spirit is invoked with the laying on of hands, in the presence of the congregation. Water provides the central symbolism for baptism. The richness of its meaning for the Christian community is suggested in the baptismal liturgy which speaks of the waters of creation and the flood, the liberation of God's people by passage through the sea, the gift of water in the wilderness, and the passage through the Jordan River to the promised land. In baptism we identify ourselves with this people of God and join the community's journey toward God. The use of water in baptism also symbolizes cleansing from sin, death to old life, and rising to begin new life in Christ. In United Methodist tradition, the water of baptism may be administered by sprinkling, pouring, or immersion. However it is administered, water should be utilized with enough generosity to enhance our appreciation of its symbolic meanings.

The baptismal liturgy includes the biblical symbol of the anointing with the Holy Spirit—the laying on of hands with the optional use of oil. This anointing promises to the baptized person the power to live faithfully the kind of life that water baptism signifies. In the early centuries of the Church, the laying on of hands usually followed immediately upon administration of the water and completed the ritual of membership. Because the laying on of hands was, in the Western Church, an act to be performed only by a bishop, it was later separated from water baptism and came to be called confirmation. In confirmation the Holy Spirit marked the baptized person as God's own and strengthened him or her for discipleship. In the worship life of the early Church, the water and the anointing led directly to the celebration of the Lord's Supper as part of the service of initiation, regardless of the age of the baptized. The current rituals of the Baptismal Covenant rejoin these three elements into a unified service. Together these symbols point to, anticipate, and offer participation in the life of the community of faith as it embodies God's presence in the world.

which are placed (open) as far apart as your learning space permits. Designate one person as "It," who calls out, "It's raining, it's raining." Everyone thinks of an animal and moves between the two umbrellas as that animal would move. The person who is "It" tries to touch one person (animal) between the two places, and then guesses the animal. Whether the guess is correct or incorrect the person touched becomes the next "It." If you will be offering the option of decorating an umbrella as part of this session (*Learn by Doing: Water,* page 51) you could use the same umbrella/s. (This activity is designed to reinforce the story used later in the session as part of *Learning and Doing, Bible Story.*)

OPENING WORSHIP

· Lesson Focus: Baptism is the sign of the new covenant.

· Light the candles: Consider saying something like: "As I light this candle let me remember - - - (It could be the same phrase each week, for example: my baptism, Jesus' baptism, God's great love for me.)

· Question: What does baptism mean?

· Response: You may wish to paraphrase something like this: "Well, now, that is a big, big question. It is just 4 words and not even big words, at that; but, just like we said in the other sessions, it will take your whole life to understand about baptism, and even then you won't have it all.

Baptism is "a sign of regeneration or the new birth," it is "a representation of the new birth in Christ Jesus and a mark of Christian discipleship." (from page 13, inside column) But what does that really mean?

Baptism is about living — it is about living with promises and responsibilities. Before the birth of

15

Jesus, God and the people of Israel promised certain things and both God and the people had responsibilities. The new covenant involves promises and responsibilities, too; it is an understanding between people and God that we have had since the death and resurrection of Jesus. In this new covenant, baptism is by water and the Spirit. Let's hear that from the Bible:

"Jesus answered, 'Very truly, I tell you, no one can enter the kingdom of God without being born of water and Spirit.'" John 3:5.

"Peter said to them, 'Repent, and be baptized every one of you in the name of Jesus Christ so that your sins may be forgiven; and you will receive the gift of the Holy Spirit.'" Acts 2:38.

This new covenant means we turn away from living for ourselves and turn toward living for God, the way Jesus taught.

It is also a way of saying you are now part of the Church, that is, you become one of the followers of Jesus. It doesn't mean just one church, like the United Methodist Church, or the Baptist Church, or the Roman Catholic Church... No, it means you're part of the whole Christian family. It's really a way of saying we're joined with Jesus and that God has blessed us.

In baptism you are promised God's love and given the responsibility to help others find that love.

How do you do all of that? You can do it through the faith that is a gift from God and from your response to God. You can do it by depending on God and believing that Jesus is with you. Here is a little bit

Baptism as Incorporation into the Body of Christ

Christ constitutes the Church as his Body by the power of the Holy Spirit (1 Corinthians 12:13, 27). The Church draws new persons into itself as it seeks to remain faithful to its commission to proclaim and exemplify the Gospel. Baptism is the sacrament of initiation and incorporation into the Body of Christ. An infant, child, or adult who is baptized becomes a member of the catholic (universal) Church, of the denomination and of the local congregation. Therefore, baptism is a rite of the whole Church, which ordinarily requires the participation of the gathered, worshiping congregation. In a series of promises within the liturgy of baptism, the community affirms its own faith and pledges to act as spiritual mentor and support for the one who is baptized. Baptism is not merely an individualistic, private, or domestic occasion. When unusual but legitimate circumstances prevent a baptism from taking place in the midst of the gathered community during its regular worship, every effort should be made to assemble representatives of the congregation to participate in the celebration. Later, the baptism should be recognized in the public assembly of worship in order that the congregation may make its appropriate affirmations of commitment and responsibility.

Baptism brings us into union with Christ, with each other, and with the Church in every time and place. Through this sign and seal of our common discipleship, our equality in Christ is made manifest (Galatians 3:27-28). We affirm that there is one baptism into Christ, celebrated as our basic bond of unity in the many communions that make up the Body of Christ (Ephesians 4:4-6). The power of the Spirit in baptism does not depend upon the mode by which water is administered, the age or psychological disposition of the baptized person, or the character of the minister. It is God's grace that makes the sacrament whole. One baptism calls the various churches to overcome their divisions and visibly manifest their unity. Our oneness in Christ calls for mutual recognition of baptism in these communions as a means of expressing the unity that Christ intends (1 Corinthians 12:12-13).

Baptism as Forgiveness of Sin

In baptism God offers and we accept the forgiveness of our sin (Acts 2:38). With the pardoning of sin which has separated us from God, we are justified–freed from the guilt and penalty of sin and restored to right relationship with God. This reconciliation is made possible through the atonement of Christ and made real in our lives by the work of the Holy Spirit. We respond by confessing and repenting of our sin, and affirming our faith that Jesus Christ has accomplished all that is necessary for our salvation. Faith is the necessary condition for justification; in baptism, that faith is professed. God's forgiveness makes possible the renewal of our spiritual lives and our becoming new beings in Christ.

Baptism as New Life

Baptism is the sacramental sign of new life through and in Christ by the power of the Holy Spirit. Variously identified as regeneration, new birth, and being born again, this work of grace makes us into new spiritual creatures (2 Corinthians 5:17). We die to our old nature which was dominated by sin and enter into the very life of Christ who transforms us. Baptism is the means of entry into new life in Christ (John 3:5; Titus 3:5), but new birth may not always coincide with the moment of the administration of water or the laying on of hands. Our awareness and acceptance of our redemption by Christ and new life in him may vary throughout our lives. But, in whatever way the reality of the new birth is experienced, it carries out the promises God made to us in our baptism.

Baptism and Holy Living

New birth into life in Christ, which is signified by baptism, is the beginning of that process of growth in grace and holiness through which God brings us into closer relationship with Jesus Christ, and shapes our

of how the United Methodist Church understands that. (Read the first three sentences under the title "The Necessity of Faith for Salvation.")"

· Music: Sing "I Belong to God" (see page 41).

· Apostles' Creed: You might wish to point out that this creed has been associated with baptism since the early church. Choose either the Traditional or Ecumenical Version (*The United Methodist Hymnal*, 881 or 882).

· Prayer: by leader or ask for a volunteer. You might use the "Prayers of the People" (*The United Methodist Hymnal*, page 879). Conclude with The Lord's Prayer (*The United Methodist Hymnal*, 894, 895, or 896).

TAKE A CLOSE LOOK

Consider the ages of the participants and the time you have for the session as you choose the amount of reading and discussing you will do. You may want to use some of these suggestions for at home preparation or follow-up study. They are also available in the Appendix for easy copying.

You may choose to read the entire portion of "By Water and the Spirit" included in Session Three *or*

Read about the various modes of baptism from *The United Methodist Book of Worship*, page 81 (third paragraph). Discuss the choices of baptism by sprinkling, pouring, or immersion. Read some or all of the scripture references.

· Discuss: when we repent, we turn away from living for ourselves and turn toward living for God. (The Greek word for 'repentance,' *metanoia*, means "a change of mind.")

I Belong to God!

· Read Genesis 17:1-14, Exodus 24:1-12, John 3:5, and Acts 2:38.

· Read The Baptismal Covenant III, *The United Methodist Hymnal*, pages 45-49.

· Keep a journal of your thoughts about baptism. You could begin by recording your thoughts about the focus statement: Baptism is the sign of the new covenant.

LEARN BY DOING

Note: all of the following suggestions are designed to enhance this study of baptism. Choose to include those that fit your time and space as well as the ages and interests of the participants. You may choose to set up learning centers (music, Bible stories, missions, water, and crafts) with a specified amount of time in each. Alternately, in each session you may plan to select several suggestions from *Learn by Doing*. Encourage all to tap into the child within and the depth of Christ in all of us. "And a child shall lead them" (Isaiah 11:6). May we grow into that which God intends!

· Music: Learn and sing "I Was There to Hear Your Borning Cry," from *The Faith We Sing*, page 2051, and create gestures to communicate words or ideas. For specific 'how to' suggestions and other music ideas see Appendix page 43.

· Bible Stories: Read the account of Noah found in Genesis. For specific 'how to' suggestions and other creative ideas for Bible stories see Appendix page 46. If you did not use the *Step into Learning* activity suggested for the opening of the session you may want to include it here, as a way to introduce the story Noah and the flood.

· Missions: Consider the responsibility you accept in baptism.

lives increasingly into conformity with the divine will. Sanctification is a gift of the gracious presence of the Holy Spirit, a yielding to the Spirit's power, a deepening of our love for God and neighbor. Holiness of heart and life, in the Wesleyan tradition, always involves both personal and social holiness.

Baptism is the doorway to the sanctified life. The sacrament teaches us to live in the expectation of further gifts of God's grace. It initiates us into a community of faith that prays for holiness; it calls us to life lived in faithfulness to God's gift. Baptized believers and the community of faith are obligated to manifest to the world the new redeemed humanity which lives in loving relationship with God and strives to put an end to all human estrangements. There are no conditions of human life that exclude persons from the sacrament of baptism. We strive for and look forward to the reign of God on earth, of which baptism is a sign. Baptism is fulfilled only when the believer and the Church are wholly conformed to the image of Christ.

Spend some time learning about missions. For specific 'how to' suggestions see Appendix page 49.

· Water: Choose from a variety of activities to learn more about and appreciate water. For specific 'how to' suggestions see Appendix page 51.

· Crafts: Consider learning and appreciating baptism through crafts. Choose from a variety of activities. For specific 'how to' suggestions see Appendix page 53.

Time of Sharing and Worship

This time can be very informal, asking those who are willing to share how they have spent their time and what they learned in the *Learn by Doing* opportunities. End your time together with a simple prayer and music. Sing "I Have Decided to Follow Jesus," *The Faith We Sing*, page 2129 or "I Belong to God" (page 41).

I Belong to God!

The Baptism of Infants and Adults

Baptism as God's Gift to Persons of Any Age

There is one baptism as there is one source of salvation—the gracious love of God. The baptizing of a person, whether as an infant or an adult, is a sign of God's saving grace. That grace—experienced by us as initiating, enabling, and empowering—is the same for all persons. All stand in need of it and none can be saved without it. The difference between the baptism of adults and that of infants is that the Christian faith is consciously being professed by an adult who is baptized. A baptized infant comes to profess her or his faith later in life, after having been nurtured and taught by parent(s) or other responsible adults and the community of faith. Infant baptism is the prevailing practice in situations where children are born to believing parents and brought up in Christian homes and communities of faith. Adult baptism is the norm when the Church is in a missionary situation, reaching out to persons in a culture which is indifferent or hostile to the faith. While the baptism of infants is appropriate for Christian families, the increasingly minority status of the Church in contemporary society demands more attention to evangelizing, nurturing, and baptizing adult converts.

Infant baptism has been the historic practice of the overwhelming majority of the Church throughout the Christian centuries. While the New Testament contains no explicit mandate, there is ample evidence for the baptism of infants in Scripture (Acts 2:38-41, 16:15,33) and in early Christian doctrine and practice. Infant baptism rests firmly on the understanding that God prepares the way of faith before we request or even know that we need help (prevenient grace). The sacrament is a powerful expression of the reality that all persons come before God as no more than helpless infants, unable to do

Session Four

Teaching Plans

LESSON FOCUS: Baptism is always a sign and means of God's grace for people of any age.

GENERAL SUPPLIES NEEDED: You will want to have large sheets of paper and markers available during each session. Supplies needed for *Learn by Doing* are listed on the Appendix pages.

PREPARATION NOTES: The opening worship includes a question and response. In this way the baptism topic for the session is considered. Choose those who will ask and respond. With coaching, a non-reader could ask the question. The one responding needs to be competent in reading and speaking. It could be a youth, older child, or an adult. Give both individuals time to prepare. Supply a visual means to identify those two, such as scarves, head bands, sashes, etc.

Display the lesson focus in your room. You may wish to make a poster, adding each session's focus as the study progresses (see Appendix page 65).

There are several opportunities during the session for music. Have someone prepared to lead.

Prepare a simple gathering area for beginning and ending each session and for any necessary announcements. Include a cross and, if possible, your congregation's baptismal font or supply a large shell. You might want to have electric or battery candles that can safely be left lit during the entire session.

Display pictures with a baptismal theme. You may have some in the picture files at your church or you may locate some online.

Prepare and have available paper/pencil/coloring sheets for use as needed at any time during the session. A word search puzzle for each session is available in the Appendix or create your own at *www.puzzle-maker.com* using the words listed on the appropriate Appendix page. The puzzle could be a cooperative time for older and younger learners. Coloring pages can be created using clip art. Look for images such as baptismal fonts, shells, boats, doves, etc.

For infants and toddlers provide water toys. You may ask parents or others to bring in items such as a water mat, plastic toy aquarium, water crib toys, toy waterfall, bath toys, bath mitts, hooded bath towels, a water play center, beach toys, water flutes or whistles, water babies (dolls to fill with warm water). Provide appropriate safety precautions and supervision.

Do you need name tags? Make sure that everyone has one, youngest to oldest!

For STEP INTO LEARNING, immediately below, you will need white feathers, available in craft stores.

STEP INTO LEARNING: *Floating Feathers.* As participants arrive, give each person a feather and ask them to remain inside the circle of chairs. Let them hold it and discuss how light in weight it is. The baptism story of Jesus includes the Holy Spirit coming to Jesus as a dove. Set

anything to save ourselves, dependent upon the grace of our loving God. The faithful covenant community of the Church serves as a means of grace for those whose lives are impacted by its ministry. Through the Church, God claims infants as well as adults to be participants in the gracious covenant of which baptism is the sign. This understanding of the workings of divine grace also applies to persons who for reasons of handicapping conditions or other limitations are unable to answer for themselves the questions of the baptismal ritual. While we may not be able to how God works in their lives, our faith teaches us that God's grace is sufficient for their needs and, thus, they are appropriate recipients of baptism.

The Church affirms that children being born into the brokenness of the world should receive the cleansing and renewing forgiveness of God no less than adults. The saving grace made available through Christ's atonement is the only hope of salvation for persons of any age. In baptism infants enter into a new life in Christ as children of God and members of the Body of Christ. The baptism of an infant incorporates him or her into the community of faith and nurture, including membership in the local church.

The baptism of infants is properly understood and valued if the child is loved and nurtured by the faithful worshiping church and by the child's own family. If a parent or sponsor (godparent) cannot or will not nurture the child in the faith, then baptism is to be postponed until Christian nurture is available. A child who dies without being baptized is received into the love and presence of God because the Spirit has worked in that child to bestow saving grace. If a child has been baptized but her or his family or sponsors do not faithfully nurture the child in the faith, the congregation has a particular responsibility for incorporating the child into its life.

Understanding the practice as an authentic expression of how God works in our lives, The United Methodist Church strongly advocates the baptism of infants within the faith community: "Because the redeeming love of God, revealed in Jesus Christ, extends to all persons and because Jesus explicitly included the children in his kingdom, the pastor of each charge shall earnestly exhort all Christian parents or guardians to present their children to the Lord in Baptism at an early age" (1992 *Book of Discipline*, par. 221). We affirm that while thanksgiving to God and dedication of parents to the task of Christian childraising are aspects of infant baptism, the sacrament is primarily a gift of divine grace. Neither parents nor infants are the chief actors; baptism is an act of God in and through the Church.

We respect the sincerity of parents who choose not to have their infants baptized, but we acknowledge that these views do not coincide with the Wesleyan understanding of the nature of the sacrament. The United Methodist Church does not accept either the idea that only believer's baptism is valid or the notion that the baptism of infants magically imparts salvation apart from active personal faith. Pastors are instructed by the *Book of Discipline* to explain our teaching clearly on these matters, so that parent(s) or sponsors might be free of misunderstandings.

The United Methodist Book of Worship contains "An Order of Thanksgiving for the Birth or Adoption of the Child" (pages 585-87), which may be recommended in situations where baptism is inappropriate, but parents wish to take responsibility publicly for the growth of the child in faith. It should be made clear that this rite is in no way equivalent to or a substitute for baptism. Neither is it an act of infant dedication. If the infant has not been baptized, the sacrament should be administered as soon as possible after the Order of Thanksgiving.

God's Faithfulness to the Baptismal Covenant

Since baptism is primarily an act of God in the Church, the sacrament is to be received by an individual only once. This position is in accord with the historic teaching of the Church universal, originating as early as the second century and having been recently reaffirmed ecumenically in *Baptism, Eucharist and Ministry*.

The claim that baptism is unrepeatable rests on the steadfast faithfulness of God. God's initiative

a time limit and explain that each person is to keep the feather up by blowing on it. The object is to be responsible for their own feather, not someone else's. The more people there are in your circle the more difficult it will become to track one feather. (This activity is designed to reinforce the Bible story used later in the session as part of *Learning and Doing*.)

OPENING WORSHIP
· Lesson Focus: Baptism is always a sign and means of God's grace for people of any age.
· Light the candles: Consider saying something like: "As I light this candle let me remember - - - (It could be the same phrase each week, for example: my baptism, Jesus' baptism, God's great love for me.)
· Question: Is there an age at which people should be baptized?
· Response: You may wish to say something like: "Is there a best age to be baptized? Is it like being pointed at and being told, "You are too young?" Or being told, "You are too old?" Is that what you think might be the situation?

Let me read something to you: "There is one baptism as there is one source of salvation — the gracious love of God. The baptizing of a person, whether as an infant or an adult, is a sign of God's saving grace. That grace — experienced by us as initiating, enabling, and empowering — is the same for all persons." (page 21)

Now, wait a minute, just think about it before you say that it couldn't be the same. True, infants aren't at the same point as adults in their faith journeys. But they are baptized because God prepares the way of faith before we even know we need it. It has to do with grace.

I Belong to God!

Do you remember our discussion of grace? It seems that we talk about it in each session. That is very interesting – it must be that grace is a part of everything about baptism.

So, God prepares the way before we even know that we need it prepared. If that is true for all ages then maybe infants, not adults, really portray baptism. After all, infants couldn't do it themselves! But, and here it is – adults sometimes THINK they can do it for themselves. Maybe if they prayed more, read the Bible often, volunteered in ways that help others, then they might earn salvation. Not so! Adults can't earn it; they have to accept that it is grace that helps everyone become what God intends.

Learning about baptism, what it means, what it is, about salvation, about God's love, about Jesus as God's own – his life, death, and resurrection, about the work of the Holy Spirit in our lives takes a whole lifetime. But, we don't have to do it alone. We are nurtured in our faith and discipleship through our homes, our neighbors, and by a faithful congregation. You were about to say Sunday school, Vacation Bible School, youth and adult groups, weren't you? They are all ways for faith development, and don't forget worship and mission.

Pretty great, and you're only baptized once. God does it right for every person's baptism! You can remember your baptism at special times, but only do it once."

· Music: Sing "I Belong to God" (see page 41).

· Apostles' Creed: You might wish to point out that this creed has been associated with baptism since the early church. Choose either the Traditional or Ecumenical Version (*The United Methodist Hymnal*, 881 or 882).

establishes the covenant of grace into which we are incorporated in baptism. By misusing our God-given freedom, we may live in neglect or defiance of that covenant, but we cannot destroy God's love for us. When we repent and return to God, the covenant does not need to be remade, because God has always remained faithful to it. What is needed is renewal of our commitment and reaffirmation of our side of the covenant.

God's gift of grace in the baptismal covenant does not save us apart from our human response of faith. Baptized persons may have many significant spiritual experiences, which they will desire to celebrate publicly in the worship life of the Church. Such experiences may include defining moments of conversion, repentance of sin, gifts of the Spirit, deepening of commitment, changes in Christian vocation, important transicomprehend tions in the life of discipleship. These occasions call not for repetition of baptism, but for reaffirmations of baptismal vows as a witness to the good news that while we may be unfaithful, God is not. Appropriate services for such events would be "Confirmation or Reaffirmation of Faith" (see Baptismal Covenant I in *The United Methodist Hymnal*) or "A Celebration of New Beginnings in Faith" (*The United Methodist Book of Worship*, pages 588-90).

· Prayer: by leader or ask for a volunteer. You might use the "Prayers of the People" (*The United Methodist Hymnal*, page 879). Conclude with The Lord's Prayer (*The United Methodist Hymnal*, 894, 895, or 896).

TAKE A CLOSE LOOK

Consider the ages of the participants and the time you have for the session as you choose the amount of reading and discussing you will do. You may want to use some of these suggestions for at home preparation or follow-up study. They are also available in the Appendix for easy copying.

You may choose to read the entire portion of "By Water and the Spirit" included in Session Four *or*

Read from the adjoining column the section titled "God's Faithfulness to the Baptismal Covenant" (page 23) *or*

Read Acts 2:38-41, 16:13-15, 30-33. These passages indicate that households of followers, which must have included children, were baptized *or*

Read and discuss the "Renunciation of Sin and Profession of Faith" as found in the baptismal covenant (*United Methodist Hymnal* page 34 - 35).

· Keep a journal of your thoughts about baptism. You could begin by recording your thoughts about the focus statement: Baptism is always a sign and means of God's grace for people of any age.

LEARN BY DOING

Note: all of the following suggestions are designed to enhance this study of baptism. Choose to include those that fit your time and space, as well as the ages and interests of the participants. You may choose to set up learning centers (music, Bible stories, missions, water, and crafts) with a specified amount of time in each. Alternately, in each session you may plan to select several suggestions from *Learn by Doing*. Encourage all to tap into the child within and the depth of Christ in all of us. "And a child shall lead them: (Isaiah 11:6). May we grow into that which God intends!

· Music: Learn "We Are God's People," from *The Faith We Sing* (page 2220), or write words to sing to a familiar melody. For specific 'how to' suggestions and other music ideas see Appendix page 43.

· Bible Stories: Read the story of the baptism of Jesus, imagining yourself there. For specific 'how to' suggestions and other creative ideas for Bible stories see Appendix page 46. If you did not use the *Step into Learning* activity suggested for the opening of the session you may want to include it here, as a way to introduce the story of Jesus' baptism.

· Missions: Consider the responsibility you accept in baptism. Spend some time learning about missions. For specific 'how to' suggestions see Appendix page 49.

· Water: Choose from a variety of activities to learn more about and appreciate water. For specific 'how to' suggestions see Appendix page 51.

· Crafts: Consider learning and appreciating baptism through crafts. Choose from a variety of activities. For specific 'how to' suggestions see Appendix page 53.

TIME OF SHARING AND WORSHIP

This time can be very informal, asking those who are willing to share how they have spent their time and what they learned in the *Learn by Doing* opportunities. End your time together with a simple prayer and music. Sing "I Have Decided to Follow Jesus," *The Faith We Sing,* page 2129 or "I Belong to God" (page 41).

Nurturing People in the Life of Faith

Nurturing Persons in the Life of Faith

If persons are to be enabled to live faithfully the human side of the baptismal covenant, Christian nurture is essential. Christian nurture builds on baptism and is itself a means of grace. For infant baptism, an early step is instruction prior to baptism of parent(s) or sponsors in the Gospel message, the meaning of the sacrament, and the responsibilities of a Christian home. The pastor has specific responsibility for this step (*Book of Discipline*, par. 439.1.b.). Adults who are candidates for baptism need careful preparation for receiving this gift of grace and living out its meaning (*The Book of Discipline*, par. 216.1.).

After baptism, the faithful Church provides the nurture which makes possible a comprehensive and lifelong process of growing in grace. The content of this nurturing will be appropriate to the stages of life and maturity of faith of individuals. Christian nurture includes both cognitive learning and spiritual formation. A crucial goal is the bringing of persons to recognition of their need for salvation and their acceptance of God's gift in Jesus Christ. Those experiencing conversion and commitment to Christ are to profess their faith in a public ritual. They will need to be guided and supported throughout their lives of discipleship. Through its worship life, its Christian education programs, its spiritual growth emphases, its social action and mission, its examples of Christian discipleship, and its offering of the various means of grace, the Church strives to shape persons into the image of Christ. Such nurturing enables Christians to live out the transforming potential of the grace of their baptism.

Session Five

Teaching Plans

LESSON FOCUS: The lifelong journey of faith begun in baptism is supported by others.

GENERAL SUPPLIES NEEDED: You will want to have large sheets of paper and markers available during each session. Supplies needed for *Learn by Doing* are listed on the Appendix pages.

PREPARATION NOTES: The opening worship includes a question and response. In this way the baptism topic for the session is considered. Choose those who will ask and respond. With coaching, a non-reader could ask the question. The one responding needs to be competent in reading and speaking. It could be a youth, older child, or an adult. Give both individuals time to prepare. Supply a visual means to identify those two, such as scarves, head bands, sashes, etc.

Display the lesson focus in your room. You may wish to make a poster, adding each session's focus as the study progresses (see Appendix page 65).

There are several opportunities during the session for music. Have someone prepared to lead.

Prepare a simple gathering area for beginning and ending each session and for any necessary announcements. Include a cross and, if pos-

I Belong to God!

sible, your congregation's baptismal font or supply a large shell. You might want to have electric or battery candles that can safely be left lit during the entire session.

Display pictures with a baptismal theme. You may have some in the picture files at your church or you may locate some online.

Prepare and have available paper/pencil/coloring sheets for use as needed at any time during the session. A word search puzzle for each session is available in the Appendix or create your own at *www.puzzlemaker.com* using the words listed on the appropriate Appendix page. The puzzle could be a cooperative time for older and younger learners. Coloring pages can be created using clip art. Look for images such as baptismal fonts, shells, boats, doves, etc.

For infants and toddlers provide water toys. You may ask parents or others to bring in items such as a water mat, plastic toy aquarium, water crib toys, toy waterfall, bath toys, bath mitts, hooded bath towels, a water play center, beach toys, water flutes or whistles, water babies (dolls to fill with warm water). Provide appropriate safety precautions and supervision.

Do you need name tags? Make sure that everyone has one, youngest to oldest!

STEP INTO LEARNING: *What's the Weather?* Ask participants to take seats in a circle as they arrive. Mention that some weather conditions call for us to respond in a certain way. The storm that struck fear into the hearts of the disciples had them

Profession of Christian Faith and Confirmation

The Christian life is a dynamic process of change and growth, marked at various points by celebrations in rituals of the saving grace of Christ. The Holy Spirit works in the lives of persons prior to their baptism, is at work in their baptism, and continues to work in their lives after their baptism. When persons recognize and accept this activity of the Holy Spirit, they respond with renewed faith and commitment.

In the early Church, baptism, the laying on of hands, and eucharist were a unified rite of initiation and new birth for Christians of all ages. During the Middle Ages in Western Europe, confirmation was separated from baptism in both time and theology. A misunderstanding developed of confirmation as completing baptism, with emphasis upon human vows and initiation into church membership. John Wesley did not recommend confirmation to his preachers or to the new Methodist church in America. Since 1964 in the former Methodist Church, the first public profession of faith for those baptized as infants has been called Confirmation. In the former Evangelical United Brethren Church, there was no such rite until union with The Methodist Church in 1968. With the restoration of confirmation— as the laying on of hands—to the current baptismal ritual, it should be emphasized that confirmation is what the Holy Spirit does. Confirmation is a divine action, the work of the Spirit empowering a person "born through water and the Spirit" to "live as a faithful disciple of Jesus Christ."

An adult or youth preparing for baptism should be carefully instructed in its life-transforming significance and responsibilities. Such a person professes in the sacrament of baptism his or her faith in Jesus Christ and commitment to discipleship, is offered the gift of assurance, and is confirmed by the power of the Holy Spirit (see Baptismal Covenant I, sections 4, 11, and 12). No separate ritual of confirmation is needed for the believing person.

An infant who is baptized cannot make a personal profession of faith as a part of the sacrament. Therefore, as the young person is nurtured and matures so as to be able to respond to God's grace, conscious faith and intentional commitment are necessary. Such a person must come to claim the faith of the Church proclaimed in baptism as her or his own faith. Deliberate preparation for this event focuses on the young person's self-understanding and appropriation of Christian doctrines, spiritual disciplines, and life of discipleship. It is a special time for experiencing divine grace and for consciously embracing one's Christian vocation as a part of the priesthood of all believers. Youth who were not baptized as infants share in the same period of preparation for profession of Christian faith. For them, it is nurture for baptism, for becoming members of the Church, and for confirmation.

When persons who were baptized as infants are ready to profess their Christian faith, they participate in the service which United Methodism now calls Confirmation. This occasion is not an entrance into Church membership, for this was accomplished through baptism. It is the first public affirmation of the grace of God in ones baptism and the acknowledgment of ones acceptance of that grace by faith. This moment includes all the elements of conversion–repentance of sin, surrender and death of self, trust in the saving grace of God, new life in Christ, and becoming an instrument of God's purpose in the world. The profession of Christian faith, to be celebrated in the midst of the worshiping congregation, should include the voicing of baptismal vows as a witness to faith and the opportunity to give testimony to personal Christian experience.

Confirmation follows profession of the Christian faith as part of the same service. Confirmation is a dynamic action of the Holy Spirit that can be repeated. In confirmation the outpouring of the Holy Spirit is invoked to provide the one being confirmed with the power to live in the faith that he or she has professed. The basic meaning of confirmation is strengthening and making firm in Christian faith and life. The ritual action in confirmation is the laying on of hands as the sign of God's continuing gift of the grace of Pentecost. Historically, the person being confirmed was also anointed on the forehead with oil in the shape of a cross as a mark of the Spirit's work. The ritual of the baptismal covenant included in *The*

calling for Jesus. Designate one person as leader, who will address each person in turn and announce the weather (rain, sun, wind, snow, cool, hot, hurricane, tornado, etc.), followed by either the question, "What will you do?" or "What won't you do?" Encourage serious as well as silly answers, such as "I will take an umbrella" or "I will stand on my head and wiggle my toes." (This activity is designed to reinforce the Bible story used later in the session as part of *Learning and Doing*.)

OPENING WORSHIP

· Lesson Focus: The lifelong journey of faith begun in baptism is supported by others.

· Light the candles: Consider saying something like: "As I light this candle let me remember - - - (It could be the same phrase each week, for example: my baptism, Jesus' baptism, God's great love for me.)

· Question: Can I travel my journey of faith alone?

· Response: You may wish to say something like: "Alone? You mean all alone? No one to help you to understand the road map? I guess my first thought is "Why would you want to?" But then, I would have to wonder if it could even be done alone. Do you remember in the last session we talked about being nurtured in our faith and discipleship through our families, our neighbors, and a faithful congregation - we don't do it alone! There is Sunday school, Vacation Bible School, youth and adult groups, worship services, and missions.

A person grows in faith and takes on Christian responsibilities. Through careful teaching and understanding, confirmation may become an opportunity to publicly profess one's faith. Infants can't say that they have faith; but, when the time is right and they have grown in faith, they may come before the congregation in confirmation.

There can also be times other than confirmation when a person shares with the faith community a sense of growth and a deepened understanding of God's will. These times can be celebrated as a reaffirmation of baptism; times to remember and celebrate, with others, God's gift of divine grace. Thanks be to God."

· Music: Sing "I Belong to God" (see page 41).

· Apostles' Creed: You might wish to point out that this creed has been associated with baptism since the early church. Choose either the Traditional or Ecumenical Version (*The United Methodist Hymnal*, 881 or 882).

· Prayer: by leader or ask for a volunteer. You might use the "Prayers of the People" (*The United Methodist Hymnal*, page 879). Conclude with The Lord's Prayer (*The United Methodist Hymnal*, 894, 895, or 896).

TAKE A CLOSE LOOK

Consider the ages of the participants and the time you have for the session as you choose the amount of reading and discussing you will do. You may want to use some of these suggestions for at home preparation or follow-up study. They are also available in the Appendix for easy copying.

You may choose to read the entire portion of "By Water and the Spirit" included in Session Five **or**

Read the sections "Profession of Christian Faith and Confirmation" (page 28) and "Reaffirmation of One's Profession of Christian Faith" **or**

United Methodist Hymnal makes clear that the first and primary confirming act of the Holy Spirit is in connection with and immediately follows baptism.

When a baptized person has professed her or his Christian faith and has been confirmed, that person enters more fully into the responsibilities and privileges of membership in the Church. Just as infants are members of their human families, but are unable to participate in all aspects of family life, so baptized infants are members of the Church—the family of faith—but are not yet capable of sharing everything involved in membership. For this reason, statistics of church membership are counts of professed/ confirmed members rather than of all baptized members.

Reaffirmation of One's Profession of Christian Faith

The life of faith which baptized persons live is like a pilgrimage or journey. On this lifelong journey there are many challenges, changes, and chances. We engage life's experiences on our journey of faith as a part of the redeeming and sanctifying Body of Christ. Ongoing Christian nurture teaches, shapes, and strengthens us to live ever more faithfully as we are open to the Spirit's revealing more and more of the way and will of God. As our appreciation of the good news of Jesus Christ deepens and our commitment to Christ's service becomes more profound, we seek occasions to celebrate. Like God's people through the ages, all Christians need to participate in acts of renewal within the covenant community. Such an opportunity is offered in every occasion of baptism when the congregation remembers and affirms the gracious work of God which baptism celebrates. Baptismal Covenant IV in *The United Methodist Hymnal* is a powerful ritual of reaffirmation which uses water in ways that remind us of our baptism. The historic "Covenant Renewal Service" and "Love Feast" can also be used for this purpose (*The United Methodist Book of Worship*, pages 288-94 and 581-84). Reaffirmation of faith is a human response to God's grace and therefore may be repeated at many points in our faith journey.

Consider this sentence from *The United Methodist Book of Worship*, pages 81-82, "While baptism signifies the whole working of God's grace, much that it signifies, from the washing away of sin to the pouring out of the Holy Spirit, will need to happen during the course of a lifetime."

Discuss these phrases from that sentence:

"whole working of God's grace"
"washing away of sin"
"pouring out of the Holy Spirit"
"course of a lifetime"

· Keep a journal of your thoughts about baptism. You could begin by recording your thoughts about the focus statement: The lifelong journey of faith begun in baptism is supported by others.

Learn by Doing

Note: all of the following suggestions are designed to enhance this study of baptism. Choose to include those that fit your time and space as well as the ages and interests of the participants. You may choose to set up learning centers (music, Bible stories, missions, water, and crafts) with a specified amount of time in each. Alternately, in each session you may plan to select several suggestions from *Learn by Doing*. Encourage all to tap into the child within and the depth of Christ in all of us. "And a child shall lead them" (Isaiah 11:6). May we grow into that which God intends!

· Music: Sing "They'll Know We Are Christians by Our Love," from *The Faith We Sing*, page 2223, and add rhythm instruments. For specific 'how to' suggestions and other music ideas see Appendix page 43.

· Bible Stories: Be on the boat with Jesus and the disciples during a storm. For specific 'how to' suggestions and other creative ideas for Bible stories see Appendix page 46. If you did not use the *Step into Learning* activity suggested for the opening of the session you may want to include it here, as a way to introduce this story.

· Missions: Consider the responsibility you accept in baptism. Spend some time learning about missions. For specific 'how to' suggestions see Appendix page 49.

· Water: Choose from a variety of activities to learn more about and appreciate water. For specific 'how to' suggestions see Appendix page 51.

· Crafts: Consider learning and appreciating baptism through crafts. Choose from a variety of activities. For specific 'how to' suggestions see Appendix page 53.

TIME OF SHARING AND WORSHIP

This time can be very informal, asking those who are willing to share how they have spent their time and what they learned in the *Learn by Doing* opportunities. End your time together with a simple prayer and music. Sing "I Have Decided to Follow Jesus," *The Faith We Sing,* page 2129 or "I Belong to God" (page 41).

Baptism in relation to other rites of the Church

The grace of God which claims us in our baptism is made available to us in many other ways and, especially, through other rites of the Church.

Baptism and the Lord's Supper
(Holy Communion or the Eucharist)

Through baptism, persons are initiated into the Church; by the Lord's Supper, the Church is sustained in the life of faith. The Services of the Baptismal Covenant appropriately conclude with Holy Communion, through which the union of the new member with the Body of Christ is most fully expressed. Holy Communion is a sacred meal in which the community of faith, in the simple act of eating bread and drinking wine, proclaims and participates in all that God has done, is doing, and will continue to do for us in Christ. In celebrating the Eucharist, we remember the grace given to us in our baptism and partake of the spiritual food necessary for sustaining and fulfilling the promises of salvation. Because the table at which we gather belongs to the Lord, it should be open to all who respond to Christ's love, regardless of age or church membership. The Wesleyan tradition has always recognized that Holy Communion may be an occasion for the reception of converting, justifying, and sanctifying grace. Unbaptized persons who receive communion should be counseled and nurtured toward baptism as soon as possible.

Baptism and Christian Ministry

Through baptism, God calls and commissions persons to the general ministry of all Christian believers (see *The Book of Discipline*, 1992, par. 101-

Session Six

Teaching Plans

LESSON FOCUS: God's grace comes to us in many ways.

GENERAL SUPPLIES NEEDED: You will want to have large sheets of paper and markers available during each session. Supplies needed for *Learn by Doing* are listed on the Appendix pages.

PREPARATION NOTES: The opening worship includes a question and response. In this way the baptism topic for the session is considered. Choose those who will ask and respond. With coaching, a non-reader could ask the question. The one responding needs to be competent in reading and speaking. It could be a youth, older child, or an adult. Give both individuals time to prepare. Supply a visual means to identify those two, such as scarves, head bands, sashes, etc.

Display the lesson focus in your room. You may wish to make a poster, adding each session's focus as the study progresses (see Appendix page 65).

There are several opportunities during the session for music. Have someone prepared to lead.

Prepare a simple gathering area for beginning and ending each session and for any necessary announcements. Include a cross and, if possible, your congregation's baptismal font or supply a large shell. You might want to have electric or battery candles that can safely be left lit during the entire session.

Display pictures with a baptismal theme. You may have some in the picture files at your church or you may locate some online.

Prepare and have available paper/pencil/coloring sheets for use as needed at any time during the session. A word search puzzle for each session is available in the Appendix or create your own at *www.puzzlemaker.com* using the words listed on the appropriate Appendix page. The puzzle could be a cooperative time for older and younger learners. Coloring pages can be created using clip art. Look for images such as baptismal fonts, shells, boats, doves, etc.

For infants and toddlers provide water toys. You may ask parents or others to bring in items such as a water mat, plastic toy aquarium, water crib toys, toy waterfall, bath toys, bath mitts, hooded bath towels, a water play center, beach toys, water flutes or whistles, water babies (dolls to fill with warm water). Provide appropriate safety precautions and supervision.

Do you need name tags? Make sure that everyone has one, youngest to oldest!

STEP INTO LEARNING: *How Much Water.* Our study of baptism has mentioned water often, because it is important in baptism! How do we use water? Designate a leader to ask water questions (found on page 39). The leader may give either a right (provided) or a wrong answer; the group considers the information

7). This ministry, in which we participate both individually and corporately, is the activity of discipleship. It is grounded upon the awareness that we have been called into a new relationship not only with God, but also with the world. The task of Christians is to embody the Gospel and the Church in the world. We exercise our calling as Christians by prayer, by witnessing to the good news of salvation in Christ, by caring for and serving other people, and by working toward reconciliation, justice, and peace in the world. This is the universal priesthood of all believers.

From within this general ministry of all believers, God calls and the Church authorizes some persons for the task of representative ministry (see *The Book of Discipline*, 1992, par. 108-10). The vocation of those in representative ministry includes focusing, modeling, supervising, shepherding, enabling, and empowering the general ministry of the Church. Their ordination to Word, Sacrament, and Order or consecration to diaconal ministries of service, justice, and love is grounded in the same baptism that commissions the general priesthood of all believers.

Baptism and Christian Marriage

In the ritual for marriage, the minister addresses the couple: "I ask you now, in the presence of God and these people, to declare your intention to enter into union with one another through the grace of Jesus Christ, who calls you into union with himself as acknowledged in your baptism" (*The United Methodist Hymnal*, page 865). Marriage is to be understood as a covenant of love and commitment with mutual promises and responsibilities. For the Church, the marriage covenant is grounded in the covenant between God and God's people into which Christians enter in their baptism. The love and fidelity which are to characterize Christian marriage will be a witness to the gospel and the couple are to "Go to serve God and your neighbor in all that you do."

When ministers officiate at the marriage of a couple who are not both Christians, the ritual needs to be altered to protect the integrity of all involved.

Baptism and Christian Funeral

The Christian Gospel is a message of death and resurrection, that of Christ and our own. Baptism signifies our dying and rising with Christ. As death no longer has dominion over Christ, we believe that if we have died with Christ we shall also live with him (Romans 6:8-9). As the liturgy of the Service of Death and Resurrection proclaims: "Dying, Christ destroyed our death. Rising, Christ restored our life. Christ will come again in glory. As in baptism (Name) put on Christ, so in Christ may (Name) be clothed with Glory" (*The United Methodist Hymnal*, page 870).

If the deceased person was never baptized, the ritual needs to be amended in ways which continue to affirm the truths of the Gospel, but are appropriate to the situation.

Committal of the deceased to God and the body to its final resting place recall the act of baptism and derive Christian meaning from God's baptismal covenant with us. We acknowledge the reality of death and the pain of loss, and we give thanks for the life that was lived and shared with us. We worship in the awareness that our gathering includes the whole communion of saints, visible and invisible, and that in Christ the ties of love unite the living and the dead.

Conclusion

Baptism is a crucial threshold that we cross on our journey in faith. But there are many others, including the final transition from death to life eternal. Through baptism we are incorporated into the ongoing history of Christ's mission, and we are identified and made participants in God's new history in

and decides if the answer given was true or false.

OPENING WORSHIP
· Lesson Focus: God's grace comes to us in many ways.
· Light the candles: Consider saying something like: "As I light this candle let me remember - - - (It could be the same phrase each week, for example: my baptism, Jesus' baptism, God's great love for me.)
· Question: Baptism is important – but are there other ways to experience and receive God's Grace?
· Response: You may wish to say something like: "I am glad that you asked that important question. Yes, there are other ways. Let's consider just a few of those times. United Methodists believe that Baptism and the Lord's Supper are the two *sacraments*, special ways we know God's loving presence. There is also the ministry of all Christians, Christian marriage, and the Christian funeral.

So, starting with the Lord's Supper: We remember God's grace being given in baptism. In fact, baptism or a reaffirmation of our baptism should be followed by a celebration of Holy Communion! Through our taking part in the Lord's Supper, we share bread and wine (or juice) with other believers. In this way we proclaim and participate in all that God has done, is doing, and will do for us in Christ. By sharing food, spiritual food of the Lord's Supper, we are given what is necessary in our salvation. We receive grace.

Several times during these sessions it has been mentioned that through baptism we take on responsibilities. That is our part of the covenant, the new covenant we have already talked about. Well, through baptism we are called to ministry. We take on a big job. Listen to this, "The task of Christians is to embody the Gospel and the Church in the world." (p. 34) Can we take the message of Jesus to the whole world? Yes, we can! Can we care for all people? We can do that, too! Not alone, of course. We have the Lord's Supper and the entire faith community to give us strength and courage and to share in the work of ministry. Kids, too? Oh, yes, especially children.

God's grace also comes to us during services of Christian marriage and Christian funerals. If we look at *The United Methodist Hymnal*, page 865, we find this statement, "- - - through the grace of Jesus Christ, - - - " and on page 871 a section of the funeral service is titled "The Word of Grace."

Baptism is just the beginning. There are many times during our journey of faith in which we experience God's grace. Jesus promised us "And remember, I am with you always, to the end of the age." (Matthew 28:20b)

· Music: Sing "I Belong to God" (see page 41).

· Apostles' Creed: You might wish to point out that this creed has been associated with baptism since the early church. Choose either the Traditional or Ecumenical Version (*The United Methodist Hymnal*, 881 or 882).

· Prayer: by leader or ask for a volunteer. You might use the "Prayers of the People" (*The United Methodist Hymnal*, page 879). Conclude with The Lord's Prayer (*The United Methodist Hymnal*, 894, 895, or 896).

Jesus Christ and the new age that Christ is bringing. We await the final moment of grace, when Christ comes in victory at the end of the age to bring all who are in Christ into the glory of that victory. Baptism has significance in time and gives meaning to the end of time. In it we have a vision of a world recreated and humanity transformed and exalted by God's presence. We are told that in this new heaven and new earth there will be no temple, for even our churches and services of worship will have had their time and ceased to be, in the presence of God, "the first and the last, the beginning and the end" (Revelation 21-22).

Until that day, we are charged by Christ to "Go therefore and make disciples of all nations, baptizing them in the name of the Father, the Son, and the Holy Spirit, and teaching them to obey everything that I have commanded you. And remember, I am with you always, to the end of the age" (Matthew 28:19-20). Baptism is at the heart of the Gospel of grace and at the core of the Church's mission. When we baptize we say what we understand as Christians about ourselves and our community: that we are loved into being by God, lost because of sin, but redeemed and saved in Jesus Christ to live new lives in anticipation of his coming again in glory. Baptism is an expression of God's love for the world, and the effects of baptism also express God's grace. As baptized people of God, we therefore respond with praise and thanksgiving, praying that God's will be done in our own lives:

"We your people stand before you
water-washed and Spirit-born.
By your grace, our lives we offer,
Recreate us; God, transform!"

Ruth Duck, "Wash, O God, Our Sons and Daughters"
(*The United Methodist Hymnal,* 605) Used with permission.

TAKE A CLOSE LOOK

Consider the ages of the participants and the time you have for the session as you choose the amount of reading and discussing you will do. You may want to use some of these suggestions for at home preparation or follow-up study. They are also available in the Appendix for easy copying.

You may choose to read the entire portion of "By Water and the Spirit" included in Session Six *or*

Read the statement found in *The United Methodist Hymnal*, page 865 at the top of the page "Declaration by the Man and the Woman, Pastor to the persons who are to marry" *or*

Read the statement found in *The United Methodist Hymnal*, page 871 at the top of the page "The Word of Grace."

Keep a journal of your thoughts about baptism. You could begin by recording your thoughts about the focus statement: God's grace comes to us in many ways.

LEARN BY DOING

Note: all of the following suggestions are designed to enhance this study of baptism. Choose to include those that fit your time and space, as well as the ages and interests of the participants. You may choose to set up learning centers (music, Bible stories, missions, water, and crafts) with a specified amount of time (or sessions) in each. Alternately, in each session you may plan to select several suggestions from *Learn by Doing*. Encourage all to tap into the child within and the depth of Christ in all of us. "And a child shall lead them" (Isaiah 11:6). May we grow into that which God intends!

· Music: Learn "Go to the World," from *Upper Room Worshipbook:*

Music and Liturgies for Spiritual Formation, page 132 (Sing to ENGELBERG, No. 131). For specific 'how to' suggestions and other music ideas see Appendix page 43.

· Bible Stories: Consider repeating one or more of the stories from previous sessions or tell one you have not had the opportunity to include in previous sessions. For specific 'how to' suggestions and other creative ideas for Bible stories see Appendix page 46. If you did not use the *Step into Learning* activity suggested for the opening of the session you may want to include it here.

· Missions: Consider the responsibility you accept in baptism. Spend some time learning about missions. For specific 'how to' suggestions see Appendix page 49.

· Water: Choose from a variety of activities to learn more about and appreciate water. For specific 'how to' suggestions see Appendix page 51.

· Crafts: Consider learning and appreciating baptism through crafts. Choose from a variety of activities. For specific 'how to' suggestions see Appendix page 53.

TIME OF SHARING AND WORSHIP

This time can be very informal, asking those who are willing to share how they have spent their time and what they learned in the *Learn by Doing* opportunities. End your time together with a simple prayer and music. Sing "I Have Decided to Follow Jesus," *The Faith We Sing,* page 2129 or "I Belong to God" (page 41).

Step into Learning

How much water?

Our study of baptism has mentioned water pretty often, because it is important. It is an important part of baptism. How do we use water?

Taking a shower - 15-30 gallons

Flushing the toilet - 2-7 gallons

Brushing teeth - 1 gallon

One person's water drinking for one day, for healthy living - 1/2 gallon

Needed to process one can of fruit or vegetables - 9.3 gallons

Needed to manufacture a new car and its four tires - 39,090 gallons

How long can a person live without water? Approximately one week, depending upon conditions

How much of the human body is water? 66%

How much of the earth's surface is water? 80%

Of all the earth's water, how much is ocean or seas? 97%

Is it possible for me to drink water that was part of the dinosaur era?
Yes - water is constantly recycled

How much does one gallon of water weigh?   8.34 pounds

How much water must a dairy cow drink to produce one gallon of milk?   Four gallons

How much water is used during the growing/production of a single orange? 13.8 gallons

Information from http://www.epa.gov/ogwdw/kids/grades_4-8_matching_game_answers.html
http://www.epa.gov/ogwdw/kids/water_trivia_facts.html

How much water is there on Earth?
There's a whole lot of water on Earth! Something like 326,000,000,000,000,000,000 gallons **(326 million trillion gallons)** of the stuff (roughly 1,260,000,000,000,000,000,000 liters) can be found on our planet. This water is in a **constant cycle** — it evaporates from the ocean, travels through the air, rains down on the land and then flows back to the ocean.

http://science.howstuffworks.com/question157.htm

I Belong to God!

I Belong to God

Marie Pooler; alt by Helen Kemp

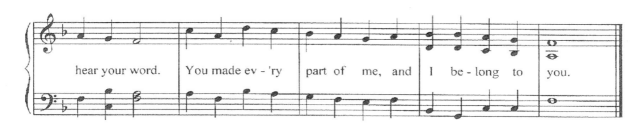

Motions: "You made every part of me" - hands on chest
"lift my voice" - point to mouth
"lift my hands" - hands outstretched
"use my eyes" - point to eyes
"use my ears" - point to ears

I Belong to God!

Learn by Doing

Music

SETUP: arrange to have a pianist and piano (or electronic keyboard). You may need *The United Methodist Hymnal*, *The Faith We Sing* and *The Upper Room Worshipbook: Music and Liturgies for Spiritual Formation*.

Music offers many ways to learn. One need not be highly skilled to learn about baptism through music. There are many ways that music enters the soul. Try some of these ideas.

Who plays an instrument? Invite them to share their music. Piano? Clarinet? Trombone? Those who play C instruments could play along with piano-accompanied hymns or other music. (Others, such as B flat clarinet or trumpet or E flat alto saxophone would need someone adept at transposing to make it possible to play along with a keyboard.) Maybe you have a guitar player or a percussionist who would be willing to contribute.

PREPARATION: extend an invitation to musicians in your congregation

Include all God's children! Keep in mind that young children can learn to play a simple melody on a keyboard. You might devote some time to teaching the first phrase (or even all) of "Make Us One" *(The Faith We Sing,* page 2224). Inquire about school-type plastic recorders. Play kazoos! Wrap a comb with wax paper; lightly touch lips to the paper and hum a melody.

SUPPLIES AND PREPARATION: make inquiries to locate those with plastic school-type recorders

Make rhythm instruments. Rhythm patterns can be tapped out using unsharpened pencils. Small stones in closed plastic cups make good shakers. Bells threaded on a string add a joyous sound. Sand paper stapled on wood blocks could sound like moving feet, or waves of water. Empty boxes make good drums. If you plan to take a collection of food staples to donate to a local soup kitchen (see *Learn by Doing: Missions*) you might include boxes of pasta. Gently tap or shake the boxes for a rhythm instrument.

SUPPLIES: pencils, small stones, plastic cups, tape, small jingle bells, sand paper, wood blocks, empty cereal boxes, boxes of pasta

Use your body for percussion. Clap hands, slap legs, finger tap puffed out cheeks, finger snaps. Use your imagination!

Add creative motions. Raise your hands high over your head. Stretch your arms out. Stand on one foot, stand on tiptoes, stand with one foot in front of the other. Look up, look left, look right, bow your head. Open your eyes wide, close your eyes, raise eyebrows, frown, smile. Express surprise, happiness, sadness. Raise or lower shoulders. Sway back and forth or side to side.

Create gestures to communicate words or ideas. Learn simple phrases in American Sign Language.

SUPPLIES: *The Joy of Signing*, Lottie L. Riekehof, Gospel Publishing House, 1985 or *Signs of Faith: God's Word of Love: Bible Verses for Preteens and Youth*, Marcia Stoner, Abingdon Press, Nashville, 2001, or check for an Internet website

I Belong to God!

Encourage original compositions. You may find musically creative people in attendance. Encourage compositions being written both during the time you are together and between sessions.

SUPPLIES: staff paper, writing supplies, Bible (optional - computer with music-writing software)

Write a rap rhythm. All God's people can take part in this activity. Very young children may recognize the rap rhythm of "Five Little Monkeys" found in children's books and recordings. Once the rhythm is shared, compose a rap using that rhythm. It doesn't even need to rhyme! When you have some words add claps, foot taps, and whatever else you think fits. Below is a sample beginning.

(Five little monkeys jumping on the bed)
All of the people come to the water

(One fell off and bumped his head)
One waded in; washed of his sin

Make up words to familiar melodies. Select a Bible passage or an idea. Choose a tune such as "Row, Row, Row Your Boat." Fit your words to the melody. Below is a sample.

(Row, row, row your boat)
Jesus came to baptism

(Gently down the stream)
Up to John he went

(Merrily, merrily, merrily, merrily)
Water, water all around

(Life is but a dream)
To us from God is sent

Select a hymn or spiritual; sing or listen to it and add creative ideas. A conversation about the text or the mood the tune evokes may be quite thought-provoking!

Music suggestions:

The United Methodist Hymnal:
- Pages 337-360
- 193, "Jesus! The Name High Over All"
- 252, "When Jesus Came to Jordan"
- 378, "Amazing Grace"
- 605, "Wash, O God, Our Sons and Daughters"

The Faith We Sing
- 2040, "Awesome God"
- 2051, "I Was There to Hear Your Borning Cry"
- 2107, "Wade in the Water"
- 2120, "Spirit, Spirit of Gentleness"
- 2122, "She Comes Sailing on the Wind"
- 2129, "I Have Decided to Follow Jesus"
- 2220, "We Are God's People"
- 2223, "They'll Know We Are Christians by Our Love"
- 2224, "Make Us One"

Upper Room Worshipbook: Music and Liturgies for Spiritual Formation
- 132, "Go to the World" (Sing to ENGELBERG, No. 131)
- 415, "Come Now, O Prince of Peace"

Learn by Doing

Bible Stories

SUPPLIES: you may need items for making and using puppets, costuming actors, writing dialog and creating scenes, a simple theater (perhaps a cardboard box), chenille stems for figures, a box of sand, boxes for dioramas, computer to make power point presentations, several basins, large shells, the baptismal font (if possible), table top continuous water fountain (available from craft or florist stores as well as some mail-order catalogues), pitchers of water, a water play table, plastic spray bottles, a wading pool, copies of sandals for each person (Appendix page 66), Bibles. FOR SAFETY HAVE ALL OPEN CONTAINERS OF WATER CONTINUOUSLY SUPERVISED.

You may want to supply these books:
1. *In the Beginning*, Stephanie Jeffs, Illustrated by Susan Wintringham, Abingdon Press
2. *Step by Step: Noah's Ark*, Leena Lane and Gillian Chapman, Barnabas Press

The biblical water stories offer many ways to learn. One need not be a trained performer or script writer to learn about baptism through drama. There are many ways that it can enter the soul. Try some of these ideas.

Select a story; read or listen to it and add your creativity. Consider making and using puppets, costumed actors, writing dialog and creating scenes, a simple theater, chenille stem figures set in a box of sand, make box dioramas of selected scenes, power point presentations, sound effects, pantomime. Include all God's children! Keep in mind that young children can usually fully take part, especially using sock or paper bag puppets with features drawn with markers. You might devote some time to teaching a phrase or motion that could be repeated several times through the story.

If you are doing the creation story from Genesis a child (or the children) might respond to "And God said," by saying "I like it!" Each time it is said they might raise the puppet high in the air. Write the creation story in a straight-forward way or use the following. Older children, youth, and adults might consider writing a more involved play with more dialog and perhaps illustrations drawn or painted.

Reader: In the beginning God created the heaven and the earth; separated the light from and the dark.
Second Reader: and God said
Reply: I like it!
Reader: God made the sky
Second Reader: and God said
Reply: I like it!
Reader: God separated the dry land from the water, and brought forth plants
Second Reader: and God said
Reply: I like it!
Reader: God made stars, sun, and moon
Second Reader: and God said

Reply: I like it!
Reader: God made birds, and fish
Second Reader: and God said
Reply: I like it!
Reader: God made the animals, and God made people
Second Reader: and God said
Reply: I like it!

You might consider using the book *In the Beginning,* The reader might use it by reading the whole book or just to show the pictures as the dialog would indicate.

If you are doing the story of the Exodus, make it dramatic by using the whole body. Step into the water by becoming the story. Ask one person to read the story of the Hebrews leaving Egypt while others become frogs (Exodus 8:1-2), then flies (Exodus 8:20-22), followed by buzzing locusts (Exodus 10:3-4); and, most especially, line up and become water. As the speaker describes it using Exodus 14:15, 21-22, the 'water' moves to the side (or to both sides) leaving a path for the speaker (representing all of the Hebrews) to walk through. The resulting chaos during the action helps us to understand the power of the story.

Enter the story of Noah and the flood by inviting pairs of participants to join hands (representing 2 animals of each kind) and walk toward a designated space representing the ark. You might outline the space by looping crepe paper streamers around chairs or you may choose something more elaborate. The preparation of the space might be done together. Make it comfortable for those of all ages by including chairs and rug pieces or a blanket on the floor. Choose one of these ways to share the story and the experience:
1.   If the story is generally known to your group, you might use a series of questions. The questions might include, "What happened in the story of Noah?" "What about the animals?" "Did it rain a lot?" "What was the sign that God gave that never again would the world be destroyed in such a way?"
2.   Read Genesis 6:11-9:17 in its entirety or use these selections: Genesis 6:11-14, 19-22, 7:4, 8:1-3, 11-12, 9:8-13.
3.   Make puppets or chenille figures as suggested in the above paragraph to tell the story.
4.   Make figures and set up scenes using suggestions and directions from the book *Step by Step.*

Consider ways in which you will use the baptism of Jesus account in the Gospels. Together you might read one or all of the accounts (Matthew 3:13-17, Mark 1:9-11, Luke 3:21-22, John 1:29-34) and decide ways in which you will be a witness. Consider ways similar to those suggested for the story Noah. Additionally, you might include or use these alternatives:
1.   Provide copies of the picture of a sandal (Appendix page 64) so that each person has one to hold. Consider together how it would have felt to have been asked to hold Jesus' sandals as he was being baptized.
2.   Have available several basins, large shells, the baptismal font (if possible), table top continuous water fountain, pitchers of water, a water play table, plastic spray bottles, a wading pool, etc. FOR SAFETY HAVE ALL OPEN CONTAINERS OF WATER CONTINUOUSLY SUPERVISED.
3.   Consider inviting your pastor to discuss baptism.

I Belong to God!

Consider dramatizing the story of Jesus calming the storm. Together you might read one or all of the accounts (Matthew 8:24-26, Mark 4:35-41, Luke 8:22-25) and decide ways in which you might join Jesus and the disciples on the boat. Consider ways similar to those suggested for the story Noah. Additionally, you might include or use these alternatives:

1.   How will you include sound effects? You might take a trip to the kitchen and gather pots and pans, lids, spoons, and aluminum foil for shaking in long strips. You could add vocal hisses for the sound of the wild waves.

2.   After reading the Bible story, invite a spontaneous drama. Consider the dramatic effect of hearing a collection of voices simultaneously, each declaring fear. The varied voice ranges of all ages each repeating, "I'm scared" would surely place your gathering in the very center of the story. Some might whisper and others might shout. The group might choose one among them to represent Jesus to give reassurance and to calm the noise and confusion. If there are infants or very young children present you may consider moderating the noise level perhaps limiting the 'wind and waves' to vocal sounds.

Has your group appreciated a particular story? Have they each created an "I am there" response? Perhaps you will want to repeat one or more. You may want to discuss the experiences in such a way that an appreciation for the importance of water and the Holy Spirit is recognized as a theme in the Bible.

Learn by Doing

Missions

SETUP: Mount sheets of paper (such as newsprint) or poster board in such a way as to be readily available for discussion notes; plan to keep them posted for the duration of the study. You will need a supply of markers. Have information available on ways your local church and conference support missions. Display pictures of missions supported by your congregation and perhaps of local members at work.

Here are some of the responsibilities we accept through our baptism to take part in caring for others:

 ♦ "According to the grace given to you, will you remain *faithful members* of Christ's holy church and serve as Christ's *representatives* in the world?" (Baptismal Covenant I, *The United Methodist Hymnal*, page 88)

 ♦ "- - - we renew our covenant faithfully to participate in the ministries of the church by our prayers, our presence, our gifts, and our service, - - -" (Baptismal Covenant II, *The United Methodist Hymnal*, page 99)

 ♦ "Will you be loyal to The United Methodist Church, and uphold it by your prayers, your presence, your gifts, and your service?" (Baptismal Covenant III, *The United Methodist Hymnal*, page 109)

Arrange to spend a short period of time with the person or persons responsible for missions in your congregation. Record and display the ways in which missions are selected. Consider how this support is part of the responsibility accepted in baptism. Discuss and list the missions supported by your local congregation and conference.

PREPARATION: Ask someone with responsibilities for missions to attend and share ways in which missions are considered and selected for support.

Consider a collection and donation for the support of persons escaping an abusive situation. Due to their privacy and safety issues the public is not invited to visit sheltered homes so contributions are made through an agency.

PREPARATION: agency contact information

Supply information (available on the Internet and through print) on the missions supported by UMCOR. (United Methodist Committee On Relief). Consider making a donation.

SUPPLIES: It would be helpful to have a computer with Internet access available, agency contact information (www.gbgm-umc.org/umcor/)

Have available a catalog for Heifer International. Discuss such questions as: How much money would we have to send? What is meant by a 'share' of an animal? Where do the animals go? How are they sent? The catalog will have pictures of animals and short stories of some recipients and the affect the gift has had on their lives and those of others in their communities. Information is also available on the Internet.

SUPPLIES: It would be helpful to have a computer with Internet access available, agency contact information, catalog (www.Heifer.org)

Have available information on Lions Clubs International and the support the organization gives to those with vision problems. Perhaps someone in your community has raised a dog that has been accepted as a service animal. They may be willing to visit and offer information.

PREPARATION: It would be helpful to have a computer with Internet access available, agency contact information, arrange the visit of a community person who has raised or uses a service animal.

Have available information on Habitat for Humanity. If there is a house being built locally, your group may want to volunteer to help.

SUPPLIES: It would be helpful to have a computer with Internet access available, agency contact information (www.habitat.org)

Consider offering to provide food and to help serve at a local soup kitchen or homeless shelter.

PREPARATION: agency contact information

Make plans to visit a nursing home. Be prepared to visit, play games, or entertain residents. Carefully prepare for how the residents may appear and respond and appropriate ways to approach. Some young children and youth have a natural way with senior citizens or people with disabilities, while others are fearful.

PREPARATION: agency contact information

Consider a collection of food and supplies for an animal shelter. You may want to plan a visit. Some places have volunteers come to assist in animal exercising and grooming; as well as to prepare a pet for socializing in a new home.

PREPARATION: agency contact information

If you will be going as a group to lend support locally, consider the following:
1. *Carefully follow guidelines established by your congregation.*
2. *Schedule with the organization*
3. *Make sign-up sheets*
4. *Discuss appropriate behavior*
5. *Clarify work expectations and time commitment*
6. *Request written permission for children and youth*
7. *Plan for adequate supervision / chaperoning for children and youth*
8. *Discuss care and compassion for others*

Learn by Doing

Water

SET-UP: A display for 'hands-on' including shells, water toys (plastic duck, boat, novelty sponge shapes), magnifying glass, prism, mist plastic spray bottle, glasses and pitcher of drinking water, umbrella, bottle of bubbles.

The Bible tells us that God created water and God saw that it was good. We know that water is necessary for life, that it is powerful, and that through baptism we are transformed. What do we know about water that helps us to understand its goodness? How can we understand its power? How necessary is it for life? Brainstorm some of these questions together. Look at the information here and choose to do some of the learning activities.

See how many of the ways we use water the group can list in a short period of time. You might ask someone to be a time-keeper and stop discussion after two minutes. Record and display the ideas. Begin the list with baptism.

SUPPLIES: a place to write and display information from discussion, such as a large piece of newsprint and markers

Make and enjoy snow cones. Someone in the congregation may have a snow cone maker that you might borrow; they are available through 'big box' stores for under $40.

SUPPLIES: snow cone maker and supplies as suggested with the machine

Plant seeds in a paper cup. You will need untreated garden seeds, potting soil, and paper cups. Beans grow rapidly. Send them home to be watered. Suggest measuring and recording the amount of water used and the amount of growth each day.

SUPPLIES: untreated garden seeds, potting soil, and paper cups, cleanup items

Purchase umbrellas or an umbrella to decorate. Novelty, party, and craft stores or catalogues offer a range of products and costs. You might just use a regular umbrella and permanent markers. You may offer each an umbrella or work together to decorate one and display it as a reminder of the class experience. If you are playing Umbrella Tag in *Step into Learning* (Session Three) as part of the same session you might choose to use the same umbrella/s.

SUPPLIES: Umbrella (or more than one) to decorate and permanent markers

Plan to participate in a water activity. Take advantage of the season and location. Will you go fishing, swimming, to the beach, water skiing, play under a water sprinkler, hold a car wash, walk in the rain, splash through water puddles, build a snowman, make snow angels, ski, snowshoe, ice skate? If you will be leaving the building, consider the following suggestions:
1.   Carefully follow guidelines established by your congregation.
2.   Schedule with any organization (such as ski resort, swimming area)
3.   Make sign-up sheets
4.   Clarify time commitment
5.   Request written permission for children and youth
6.   Provide adequate supervision and safety precautions

I Belong to God!

Discuss and experience the various forms of water. Have available ice cubes, water in a child size plastic wading pool placed on a plastic table cloth (choose one that wouldn't be slippery for wet feet) WITH CONTINUOUS ADULT SUPERVISION, a table model mist vaporizer and a container of snow (or frost from a freezer). Arrange the items for easy accessibility for all ages and physical conditions. You may need towels!

SUPPLIES: ice cubes, wading pool, plastic table cloth, a table model mist vaporizer, container of snow (or frost from a freezer)

For an at home, snow-area learning activity, preserve a snow flake. The directions may be found at *www.northstar.k12.ak.us/schools/joy/creamers/water/snowflake.html* or by searching "preserve a snowflake."

Make a water wheel. You need two paper or plastic plates, a stapler, pencil or dowel, scissors, small paper or plastic cups (bathroom size), and string. Prepare the plates by 'nesting' them together and make holes through the centers (the point of a scissors works well). Hold one of the plates as you would if you were filling it with food. Instead, staple as many of the cups as will fit around the edge with the cup openings all toward the outside edge of the plate. Then, staple the second plate to the cups, making them secure between the two plates. As with the first plate, the cups will be attached to the 'food' side. Push the pencil or dowel through the holes in the plates. Hold the wheel loosely by holding both ends of the pencil or dowel with both hands under a stream of water. If it doesn't immediately turn enlarge the holes slightly and be sure the grasp is loose. You might experiment with your wheel to determine the amount of weight it will lift by tightly winding and tying string to the pencil or dowel and the other end to an object, such as several paper clips. (Similar instructions may be found at *http://tech.worlded.org/docs/lowell/waterwheel1.htm*)

SUPPLIES: two paper or plastic plates, a stapler, pencil or dowel, scissors, small paper or plastic cups (bathroom size), string, paper clips

Mark the water level in a container and set it in a place where it will not be disturbed between sessions. Notice the amount of water that evaporates during the interval of days.

SUPPLIES: clear glass or plastic container marked up the side in one half inch measures, water

How strong is water? Fill a glass with water, way up to the top. Rub a paperclip against your skin; the oil from you skin keeps the water from sticking to the clip. Very gently lower the clip to the surface of the water to see it float. For those interested in understanding why it floats research can be done on the Internet using "water surface tension" in the search.

SUPPLIES: drinking glass, water, paperclip

Lightly dampen a coffee filter with water. Add paint of various colors to the filter and watch them spread.

SUPPLIES: coffee filters, tempera or water-based paint, brushes

Learn by Doing

Crafts

Put the hands to work and learn! One need not be an accomplished artist to learn about baptism through crafts. There are many ways that it can enter the soul. Try some of these ideas.

Fingerpaint with whipped topping or pudding: beautiful and tasty! Using powdered (made according to the box directions using slightly less liquid) or prepared whipped dessert topping or pudding mix and blue food color imagine with hands the "feel" of water as God created our world. Provide individual sheets of paper or a mural of one long sheet for everyone to share. Left-over partial rolls of wallpaper make a good background for this project. It is easy to prepare, a good weight and, with newspaper spread on the table, easy to clean up. Drying time depends upon the thickness of the 'paint.'

SUPPLIES: whipped topping or pudding (either prepared or dry), any other ingredients needed to mix if dry, blue food coloring, paper

Make a rainbow. Begin by drawing the outline on a large sheet of heavy cardboard. There are a variety of ways you might fill it in: crayons, markers, chalk (finish with a light coating of hair spray to lesson the rubbing off), or paint. To give a dimensional effect, use colored tissue or crepe paper cut or torn in small squares, wrap around a pencil eraser (or crumple into a small ball), dip in glue, and stick it to the form.

SUPPLIES: cardboard, crayons, markers, chalk, paint, crepe or tissue paper, pencils, glue or hair spray

Rainsticks can be made using the cardboard tubes from wax paper, aluminum foil, or gift wrap. Around the spiral seam of the tube make pencil marks at intervals. Gently poke one inch nails at these marks, making sure they do not go all the way through the tube. Cover the nails by wrapping the tube with tape. *Or,* use a wire coil made from 18 gauge wire (available in craft stores). Simply wind the wire into a spring-like coil using something like a broom handle. Slip the coil inside the tube and attach the wire ends to the ends of the tube. Then, regardless of which first step you've chosen, cut two circles about an inch larger than the tube openings and securely tape one end closed. Place small stones in the tube to get the sound you like; experiment by holding your hand over the open end and turning the tube end for end to hear the sound of rain. When you get the desired sound, cover the second opening. You might decorate the tube by coloring it with markers, paint, or crayons or glue paper to it. The rainstick is a South African instrument. (Similar instructions may be found at *http://www.exploratorium.edu/ frogs/rain_stick/index.html*)

SUPPLIES: cardboard tubes from wax paper, aluminum foil, or gift wrap, nails (if using one half inch intervals on a cardboard tube you will need about 60 for each) or 18 gauge wire and wire cutter, small stones, and tape

Remember your baptism. Ask participants to bring photographs of baptisms, if available (scan or photocopy rather than using the originals). Make a large poster displaying pictures of baptism shared by those participating in the study. You might add pictures from old Sunday school story papers, from church photos or hand-drawn. Clip-art of baptismal fonts could be included.

SUPPLIES: Poster and collage material, pictures of baptism, newspapers and news magazines

Make a reminder of your baptism to wear or display. You will need pin backings (available from craft stores) and a variety of craft material - clay, old magazines for pictures, papier mache, patterns of doves, fonts, water, etc. If you are using clay you may want to have paint available during a later session, once the objects have

SUPPLIES: Clay, pictures, papier mache, various other craft materials, pin backings. (Clay can be made by mixing 2 parts flour to 1 part salt, add water for desired consistency, optional food coloring)

Make a collection of headlines from news reports that indicate our need of God's grace of salvation. You might keep in mind that the ways we mistreat the environment are sinful as are the ways we treat each other.

SUPPLIES: Newspapers and current newsmagazines. You may wish to use poster board, newsprint or a tri-fold display board for mounting your collection.

Make origami doves and boats. From the Internet you will find examples and directions for both patterns (dltk-bible.com or peacepals may be good places to start). Enter "origami dove" or "origami boat" as search phrases. Display your items as a mobile using string and coat hangers.

SUPPLIES: Origami paper and folding directions (Internet or craft book), coat hangers and string for creating a mobile

Make a window 'sun catcher' using simulated liquid leading and liquid "stained glass," available in craft stores. You will need a pattern to place beneath your work surface. Pictures of shells, baptismal fonts, or a dove are appropriate to the baptism study. You could make your patterns from pictures from old Sunday school curriculum, clip art, or baptism greeting cards. A clear plastic lid easily serves as a work surface and contains any mess. The work will take more than one session as it needs drying time. Follow the directions on the leading and color containers. Provide adequate supervision for younger participants!

SUPPLIES: liquid leading and liquid coloring, available in craft stores, pictures appropriate for baptism, clear plastic lids

Make a baptism box diorama (also suggested in *Learn by Doing, Bible Stories*). Several people could work on a shoe box diorama or larger boxes could be used to model several scenes. Make a scene for each of the Bible stories used in the study (God's creation of water, the Exodus story, the flood, Jesus baptism, Jesus calms the water) and add a modern baptism scene. Create figures from chenille stems. Use your imagination or consult the directions in *Step by Step: Noah's Ark*. An alternative to the open box diorama is a closed box with a cut out opening of about 2 inches to look through.

SUPPLIES: boxes, construction paper, glue, scissors, you may wish to use illustrations from old Sunday school curriculum or Christian magazines, clip art, or baptism greeting cards

Make candy shells. Press into a shell shaped rubber candy mold a combination of 3 ounces cream cheese and 3 cups powdered sugar (kneaded until pie dough consistency), flavor and color to your preference. Remove immediately from mold onto wax paper.

SUPPLIES: shell rubber mold (available with cake decorating supplies), cream cheese, powdered confectioners sugar, flavoring, food color, wax paper

For those interested in needle crafts appropriate for baptism, patterns for counted cross-stitch, embroidery, and latch hook may be found in stores where needle craft supplies are available.

SUPPLIES: will depend on the project selected. You may want to make plans during one session and collect the supplies in preparation for use in another.

Consider making banners for baptism.

SUPPLIES: will depend on the size, style, and intended use. You may want to make plans during one session and collect the supplies in preparation for use in another. You may wish to supply fabric scraps, fabric paint, small shells, ribbon, etc.

Take a Close Look

By Water and the Spirit: A United Methodist Understanding of Baptism, adopted by the 1996 General Conference of The United Methodist Church is available from http://www.gbod.org/worship/articles/water_spirit/ (note: between 'water' and 'spirit' is a single underline, no spaces)

The document is divided in these six parts:

Intro
We are Saved by God's Grace
The Means by Which God's Grace Comes to us
Baptism & the Life of Faith
Baptism in Relation to Other Rites of the Church
Conclusion

Session One

· Either read the Introduction of *By Water and the Spirit: A United Methodist Understanding of Baptism* or select from the following two suggestions:

1. Read the fourth paragraph beginning "Baptism for Wesley, therefore, was - - - "
2. Read the last three paragraphs of the introduction.

· Read The United Methodist Hymnal—p. 32, "Concerning the Services of the Baptismal Covenant."

· Read The Baptismal Covenant I, *The United Methodist Hymnal*, pages 33-39.

· Keep a journal of your thoughts about baptism. You could begin by recording your thoughts about the focus statement for Session One: Baptism identifies us as people for whom Jesus Christ lived, died, and was resurrected.

Session Two

· Either read *By Water and the Spirit: A United Methodist Understanding of Baptism* "We Are Saved by God's Grace" and "The Means by Which God's Grace Comes to Us" or select from the following two suggestions:

1. Read from the phrase immediately before the heading "The Necessity of Faith for Salvation." It begins "- - - grace motivates us to repentance - - - ." Continue by reading the first two sentences beneath that heading.
2. Read the second and third paragraphs of the section "The Means by Which God's Grace Comes to Us."

· If you didn't read The United Methodist Hymnal—p. 32 during the previous session do so now.

· Read The Baptismal Covenant II, *The United Methodist Hymnal*, pages 39-44.

· Keep a journal of your thoughts about baptism. You could begin by recording your thoughts about the focus statement for Session Two: Grace is God's free gift.

Session Three

· Read *By Water and the Spirit: A United Methodist Understanding of Baptism* "Baptism and the Life of Faith," through the section "Baptism and Holy Living."

· Read about the modes of baptism from *The United Methodist Book of Worship*, page 81 (third paragraph). Consider baptism by sprinkling, pouring, or immersion. Read some or all of the scripture references.

· What does it mean to say "When we repent, we turn away from living for ourselves and turn toward living for God"?

· Read Genesis 17:1-14, Exodus 24:1-12, John 3:5, and Acts 2:38.

· Read The Baptismal Covenant III, *The United Methodist Hymnal*, pages 45-49.

· Keep a journal of your thoughts about baptism. You could begin by recording your thoughts about the focus statement for Session Three: Baptism is the sign of the New Covenant.

Session Four

· Either read *By Water and the Spirit: A United Methodist Understanding of Baptism* beginning with "Baptism as God's Gift to Persons of Any Age" (under the heading "Baptism and the Life of Faith") and reading through "God's Faithfulness to the Baptismal Covenant" or read only the section titled "God's Faithfulness to the Baptismal Covenant".

· Read Acts 2:38-41, 16:13-15, 30-33, and 1 Corinthians 1:16. These passages indicate that households of followers, which must have included children, were baptized.

· Read and discuss "Renunciation of Sin and Profession of Faith" found in the baptismal covenant (*The United Methodist Hymnal* pages 34-35).

· Keep a journal of your thoughts about baptism. You could begin by recording your thoughts about the focus statement for Session Four: Baptism is always a sign and means of God's grace for people of any age.

Session Five

· Either read *By Water and the Spirit: A United Methodist Understanding of Baptism*, "Nurturing Persons in the Life of Faith" (under the heading "Baptism and the Life of Faith") through "Reaffirmation of One's Profession of Christian Faith" or read only the sections "Profession of Christian Faith and Confirmation" and "Reaffirmation of One's Profession of Christian Faith."

· Consider this sentence from *The United Methodist Book of Worship*, pages 81-82: "While baptism signifies the whole working of God's grace, much that it signifies, from the washing away of sin to the pouring out of the Holy Spirit, will need to happen during the course of a lifetime."

Consider these phrases from that sentence:
1. whole working of God's grace
2. washing away of sin
3. pouring out of the Holy Spirit
4. course of a lifetime

· Keep a journal of your thoughts about baptism. You could begin by recording your thoughts about the focus statement for Session Five: The lifelong journey of faith begun in baptism is supported by others.

Session Six

· Read *By Water and the Spirit: A United Methodist Understanding of Baptism* "Baptism in Relation to Other Rites of the Church" and "Conclusion."

· Read the statement found in *The United Methodist Hymnal*, page 865 at the top of the page "Declaration by the Man and the Woman, Pastor to the persons who are to marry."

· Read the statement found in *The United Methodist Hymnal*, page 871 at the top of the page "The Word of Grace."

· Keep a journal of your thoughts about baptism. You could begin by recording your thoughts about the focus statement for Session Six: God's grace comes to us in many ways.

Word Search, Session One

```
S   N   Y   T   M   Q   X   M   O   G   W   O
N   O   I   S   S   I   M   W   M   O   T   O
X   R   E   Y   I   P   U   C   H   D   T   A
X   E   Y   L   T   G   V   R   C   F   I   E
S   Y   T   M   P   F   S   E   P   T   R   C
U   A   S   D   A   A   Z   A   N   R   I   A
S   R   D   L   B   W   T   T   C   V   P   R
E   P   W   E   A   O   M   I   U   J   S   G
J   K   U   Q   Q   M   S   O   N   A   I   A
Y   Q   U   Y   B   U   I   N   S   D   V   J
O   I   R   E   M   X   V   N   U   L   N   M
J   V   I   Y   X   R   E   T   A   W   F   Z
```

animals	mission	baptism	music	Creation	prayer
God	Spirit	grace	water	Jesus	

Puzzle made at www.puzzle-maker.com
"I Belong to God!" © 2007 Carolyn K. Tanner. Reproduced with permission.

Word Search, Session Two

```
Y   D   H   Y   Q   U   A   S   W   E   Z   S   G   X
D   O   E   Z   R   C   M   V   A   Z   N   R   J   C
E   G   B   Z   I   R   F   O   I   A   A   S   G   K
A   H   R   D   J   E   E   T   I   C   B   M   Y   N
J   B   E   F   T   A   F   T   E   B   P   U   E   O
S   Y   W   Z   L   T   S   U   P   A   W   S   V   I
D   R   S   M   X   I   V   R   S   P   A   I   O   S
O   D   O   X   R   O   Q   Z   R   T   T   C   L   S
T   C   Q   H   A   N   T   W   A   I   E   E   F   I
N   T   C   E   W   A   T   E   R   S   R   K   X   M
J   E   S   U   S   A   N   E   N   M   L   D   Z   O
G   O   C   C   R   E   Y   A   R   P   H   O   O   W
S   H   O   L   Y   S   P   I   R   I   T   S   B   G
A   M   Z   E   X   O   D   U   S   N   T   E   B   D
\
```

baptism	Jesus	Christians	love	Creation	mission
Exodus	music	God	prayer	grace	water
Hebrews					

Word Search, Session Three

O Y V S E S I M O R P I Z Z

L P V C L V B R K G R D R Z

T N A N E V O C T H T A R Q

K U M B R E L L A W T J L A

I S R A E L J K D K E R G B

Z Y D H U I N I A R B N I E

B A R K P G A B V O Z V V B

X Z P I H S E L P I C S I D

Y C L I N U H Q P C C O R T

Y T I L I B I S N O P S E R

Y C M V X X G M S G O K W R

U F M J M G Y K I O Q N F W

C H R I S T I A N K O J V B

U E Z D L V N A M B P V P U

| ark | Israel | birth | promises | Christian | rain |
| covenant | responsibility | | discipleship | umbrella | |

Puzzle made at www.puzzle-maker.com

Word Search, Session Four

```
V  F  E  A  T  H  E  R  S  K  U  K
G  T  E  V  O  L  J  R  U  W  E  X
B  A  N  L  D  S  D  H  Q  G  O  B
G  D  G  C  N  A  X  D  A  Q  L  H
E  U  I  C  W  L  N  L  O  D  D  J
C  L  S  H  A  V  K  I  E  W  M  X
Y  T  G  T  G  A  B  H  A  W  S  I
O  T  R  F  A  T  P  C  S  S  N  E
U  L  A  H  R  I  F  N  J  F  J  V
N  L  C  K  X  O  W  V  A  H  R  O
G  L  E  B  G  N  C  N  Q  A  Q  D
H  T  U  O  Y  P  T  J  O  R  N  X
```

adult	love	age	old	child	salvation
dove	sign	feathers	young	grace	youth
infant					

Word Search, Session Five

```
Y   W   Z   T   C   N   I   D   C   W   U   X

C   I   H   A   B   O   B   F   B   L   D   A

G   N   H   N   G   I   O   Y   Q   U   U   I

N   D   G   W   H   T   I   A   F   Y   T   S

O   N   W   U   R   A   M   V   O   E   W   R

L   C   S   V   B   M   L   J   A   N   E   E

E   N   U   S   H   R   X   E   G   R   A   H

F   J   C   O   N   I   A   R   Q   U   T   T

I   J   T   M   C   F   V   G   D   O   H   O

L   G   G   X   O   N   U   E   M   J   E   V

K   J   J   P   O   O   Z   G   J   I   R   L

S   N   O   W   L   C   C   V   E   Y   H   O
```

confirmation	others	cool	rain	faith	snow
hot	sun	journey	weather	lifelong	wind

Puzzle made at www.puzzle-maker.com
"I Belong to God!" © 2007 Carolyn K. Tanner. Reproduced with permission.

Word Search, Session Six

```
U   Y   U   B   M   A   R   R   I   A   G   E   T
C   N   J   H   M   Z   Q   Z   R   F   C   R   N
B   O   W   W   P   T   B   E   G   O   P   N   U
H   I   O   N   F   D   T   R   M   B   T   F   O
T   T   R   G   L   A   X   M   C   T   R   E   M
K   A   L   S   W   A   U   T   K   B   C   Y   A
Z   V   D   P   L   N   R   O   D   A   E   R   B
A   L   H   C   I   X   W   E   R   T   F   T   C
P   A   F   O   R   W   X   G   N   S   L   S   A
F   S   N   E   C   I   U   J   A   U   S   I   R
F   A   W   W   U   S   K   Z   O   X   F   N   E
X   M   M   S   S   O   V   O   A   Z   D   I   S
L   R   X   B   A   P   T   I   S   M   J   M   G
```

amount	juice	baptism	marriage	bread	ministry
care	salvation	water	funeral	world	communion
grace					

Puzzle made at www.puzzle-maker.com
"I Belong to God!" © 2007 Carolyn K. Tanner. Reproduced with permission.

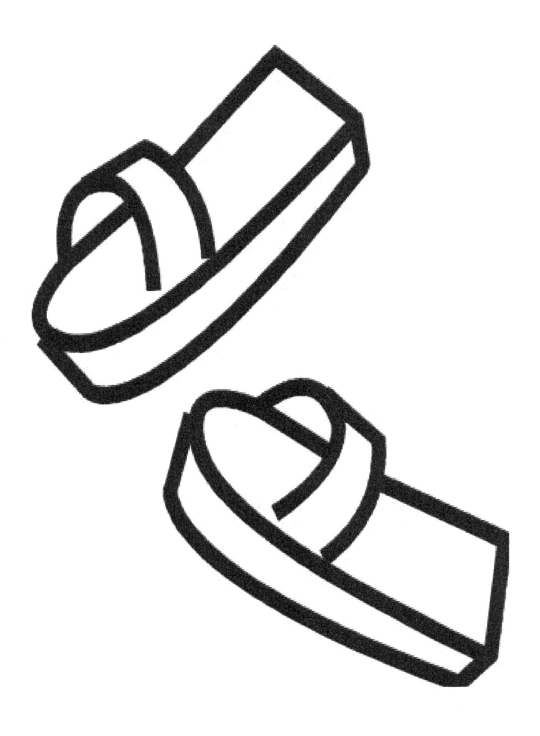

Baptism identifies us as people for whom Jesus Christ lived, died, and was resurrected.

grace
is God's
free gift.

Baptism is the sign of the New Covenant.

Baptism is always

A SIGN AND MEANS

of God's grace
for people
of any age.

The lifelong journey of faith begun in baptism is supported by others.

God's grace comes to us in MANY ways.